FULT[ON]

Salem

SHARP

I Z A R D

O N E

INDEPENDENCE

CLEBURNE

WHITE

Viola
Myatt
Sandersville
South
D0919736
ures
Wild Cherry
Union
Grooms Mill
Grangeville
Ash Flat
Opposition
Pineville
Wideman
Strawberry
Kings Mills
Sitka
Violet Hill
Franklin
Center
Hillton
Newburgh
Jones R.
Calico Rock
Piney Fk.
La Crosse
Evening Shade
Poughkeepsie
Melbourne
Sidney
Big
Galamine
Mount Olive
Lunenburgh
Maxville
Polk Bayou
Reeds Cr.
Reeds
Strawber
nore
Barren Fork
Curia
Ha
Black Oak
Hickory Valley
Mountain View
Convenience
Pleasant Valley
Riggsville
BuckHorn
Graham
Sharps Cross Roads
Walnut Grove
White R.
Batesville
Sulphur Rock
Coon Creek
Alderbrook
Big Bottom
Wolf Bayou
Salido Cr.
Wolf Bayou
Oil Trough
Banner
Floral
Bayou Departee
Kinderhook
Pleasant Plains
SOUTHERN
Red River
Olyphant
Coffeyville
J
Little Red R.
Denmark
Hiram
Judson
Bradford
Quitman
Stevens Cr.
Russell Plants P.O.
Rose Bud
Mt. Pisgah
Clear Water
Bald Knob
Turnip
Centre Hill
Judsonia
Mt. Vernon
Searcy
Bennett

Life in the Leatherwoods

John Quincy Wolf, Sr.

Life in the Leatherwoods

John Quincy Wolf

Edited, with an afterword, by John Quincy Wolf, Jr.
Introduction and notes by F. Jack Hurley
Drawings by Jim Barnett

Memphis State University Press

Library of Congress Cataloging in Publication Data

Wolf, John Quincy, 1864–1949.
  Life in the Leatherwoods.

  Autobiographical.
  Includes bibliographical references.
  1. Wolf, John Quincy, 1864–1949.   2. Ozark Mountain region
—Social life and customs.
  I. Wolf, John Quincy, 1901–1972, ed.   II. Title.
F417.09W64   1974   917.67'26'0350924 [B]   74–3412
ISBN 0–87870–020–X
ISBN 0–87870–021–8 (pbk.)

The endpaper maps are detached from O. W. Gray and Sons' National Atlas *(Philadelphia, 1876) and are reproduced courtesy of the Mississippi Valley Collection of the John Willard Brister Library at Memphis State University.*

Introduction

It is not often that the student of social history or regional literature comes in contact with an unpublished manuscript of reminiscences which stretches back over one hundred years and describes a society which, for all practical purposes, no longer exists. *Life in the Leatherwoods* is an unusual book for this and several other reasons. It is a true glimpse at social patterns among the independent hill farmers of the Arkansas Ozarks in the 1870s and 1880s. It provides the reader with a new basis for understanding frontier humor and optimism. The later chapters on steamboating give us new information on the social and economic factors involved in early regional development, and, best of all, it gives the modern reader access to the work of a great regional writer and stylist, John Quincy Wolf, Sr., as edited and completed by his son, the late John Quincy Wolf, Jr.

The elder Wolf, usually called John Q. by his friends, was born in the upper White River country of Arkansas in 1864, grew up in the deep rural isolation of that area, and eventually went on to become a banker and one of the leading citizens of Batesville, Arkansas. A man of broad interests, he built a fine home and even finer library. In 1931, approaching retirement age, he began to write short pieces for the local newspaper, the Batesville *Guard-Record*. The sketches were well received locally and some were even carried by the state's most important newspaper, the *Arkansas Gazette*. It is probable that the elder Wolf considered publishing a book, but his real talent lay in the short sketches and the book-length manuscript never emerged. At his death in 1949 a great mass of notes, fragments, clippings and short reminiscences remained, but no book. Fortunately his son was uniquely suited to the job of editing and collating his father's work.

John Quincy Wolf, Jr., called Quincy by his friends to distinguish him from his father, was a trained and disciplined scholar. His doctorate from Johns Hopkins was in the field of English literature. His life was devoted to the teaching of college level English, a career which began at Arkansas College in 1923 and continued through many years at Southwestern at Memphis until his retirement in 1971. A rigorous and precise technician, he taught three generations of students to love and respect their mother tongue. The students worked for him, but they also loved him. Over the years, he published numerous scholarly articles in two major fields, the English romantic poets and American folk music. Before his death in 1972, he had achieved international recognition for his researches in Southern regional folksongs.

During the last several years of his life, Dr. Wolf found himself increasingly incapacitated by arthritis. No longer able to go out into the hills that he loved to seek the rare and beautiful songs of the Ozarks, he turned to the long-postponed task of editing his father's notes into a book. Between painfully delivered lectures and carefully graded papers, Quincy and his wife, Bess, sorted and classified the stories. Where there were gaps, they checked with older living members of the family and gradually *Life in the Leatherwoods* emerged. The finished product was, therefore, actually the work of two minds. The words, the anecdotal style and the point of view of the elder John Q. Wolf were carefully preserved, but the whole body of work was subjected to the discipline and academic training of Professor J. Q. Wolf, Jr.

An analysis of the book itself shows that the cross-generation collaboration worked well. *Life in the Leatherwoods* plunges deeply into the rich and earthy patterns of human existence in nineteenth century rural America. There is humor on several levels. The offhand humor of the frontier shows clearly when a cow jumps off a ferry into the White River and the boatman shouts, "Go to Hell, you Campbellite!" in a reference to the Campbellite religious sect's belief in total immersion in baptism. There are stories of practical jokers who enlivened the dull routine of rural life. Most of all, the book abounds with the classic rural humor which is gently aimed at self. The senior Wolf saw much that was genuinely funny about his early life and he told his stories with gusto. This sort of humor—the country boy who looks and acts oddly but who is actually an intelligent and able young man—is perhaps the most basic theme of nineteenth century American humor, whether one is talking about the Jack Tales or Crockett's Almanacs.*

*American Jack tales have been extensively collected, especially in western North Carolina by Richard Chase and his co-workers. These

Life in the central Ozarks was not continuously humorous, of course. There was always the possibility of tragedy. The elder Wolf grew up in the hard times which immediately followed the national trauma of civil war. He heard the stories of the lawless bands of raiders known as Jayhawkers who plundered his region in the years just before his birth. He learned, as did most frontier folk, to accept the realities of death very early in his life. His terse description of his own matter-of-fact reactions to his mother's funeral provide the social historian with one of the most remarkable insights into early rural attitudes in the entire book. For the literary critic, this open acceptance of all of life, including death, lies at the heart of the senior J. Q. Wolf's value as a storyteller.

He was a keen observer of life. The structure of early Ozark society shows through clearly at many points. The church and the school were central meeting places where young Johnny Wolf and his contemporaries met to show off new finery, to compete and occasionally to fight. The coming of a visitor from out of the region became a social event to be talked about for weeks by people who were normally isolated from outside influences. Ozark farming is discussed at many points. Folk beliefs, superstitions and medicines all play an integral part of the stories and contribute to the total picture of early Ozark life. Finally, the last section, a short series of reminiscences of steamboating on the upper White River, provides one of the few glimpses we have of that industry before the advent of railroads in the region forced the high-decked steamers into oblivion.

All this is to suggest that *Life in the Leatherwoods* can be read on several levels. There is rich source material for the social historian

---

are indigenous folk tales with European antecedents, usually built on the theme of a lazy country boy who wins a variety of contests (with giants, kings, etc.) through wit and cunning. See Richard Chase's *The Jack Tales* (Boston, Houghton Miflin, 1943).

Crockett's Almanacs were published from 1835 to 1840 and were one of the most widely read early forms of popular literature in America. Written by a number of commercial writers who signed themselves "David Crockett, esq.," the almanacs with their broadly drawn characters and pseudo-heroic exploits came to represent the essence of frontier humor for thousands of Americans. See *The Crockett Almanacs*, Nashville series, 1835-1838, edited with an introduction by Franklin J. Meine and with a note on their humor by Harry J. Owens (Chicago, Caxton Club, 1955). For a discussion of Crockett's almanacs as a form of popular literature see Russel Nye's *The Unembarrassed Muse* (New York, The Dial Press, 1970), pages 282-283.

and the student of American regional literature. There is value, too, for the professional folklorist; but most of all, the book is a series of stories, well told by one of the region's finest early writers and honed into a unit by his son. John Q. Wolf and his son, Quincy, were strong men who loved life and loved to laugh. Most of all they meant this book to be enjoyed.

F. Jack Hurley

Table of Contents

List of Illustrations

Chapter I
Life in the Leatherwoods

I was born in two counties, Izard and Stone. To steal a leaf from an Indiana humorist—when I reached manhood a dispute arose between the two counties over which county could rightfully claim me as a native son. The people of Izard County insisted that I was born in Stone, whereas the Stone Countians maintained with equal vigor that I was not born in Stone but in Izard. As a matter of fact, I was born in both. My birthplace, the Wolf farm on the upper White River near Calico Rock, was in Izard, but some years later became a part of Stone County.

For fear of exaggerating or of being accused of doing so, I prefer to have a visitor to my native corner of the Ozarks describe its outstanding scenic feature. In 1818 and 1819 Henry Rowe Schoolcraft, renowned scientist and world traveler, made an exploratory trip by canoe down the White River through the Arkansas Ozarks and kept a diary of his travels which was published in book form in this country and in England. At this early date the vast territory of the Louisiana Purchase had not been legally opened to settlers, though there were a few hunters and even fewer pioneer families along the River. Schoolcraft explains that he began his journey in the highlands of southern Missouri at a point where other travelers turn back, and headed for the rugged White River country to the south.

On January 16, 1819 [he writes], a sudden turn in the River brought us in full sight of the picturesque, elevated, and precipitous bluff called the Calico Rock. This presents a most imposing facade on which are observable the imitative forms of fantastic architectural devices. It is one of those rare and fanciful works which are seldom met with and is approached under circumstances well calculated to heighten the effect of a scene in itself very striking and picturesque. As we turned a bend, suddenly the rock appeared before us at a distance of 600 yards and seemed, as we glided toward it, to present a barrier to the progress of the river. It is a lofty wall of stratified limestone, presenting a diversity of color in squares, stripes, spots, or angles, all confusedly mixed and arranged according to the inimitable pencil of nature, and hence its name. It is overlaid by a stratum of ochreous clays and red and greenish colored earths full of ferruginous particles, which have been washed by rains into the crevices of stone and thence oozing down the surface have communicated to it different colors. These have been in some degree altered, variegated, or set by the acids and juices of oak and other leaves, giving the rock a singular appearance, which the German mineralogists term tarnished colors (*angelaufenen farben*). This species of scenery is peculiar to the American landscape. Nothing of the kind marks the banks of the Rhine so much eulogized by travelers.*

Across the River from the one-room log cabin where I was born and where I lived during my first six years the magnificent Calico Rock, which had so strongly impressed Schoolcraft, rose sheer three hundred feet into the air, with its vast shoulders sloping gently away to the east and west. Altogether it was a mile long. Because of its fantastic designs of yellow, blue, green, black, light gray, bronze, and various shades of iron-red, the early frontiersmen had named it after the popular cloth for women's dresses, which in that day was often variegated in color. From every part of our hundred-acre farm that ran from the river bank back to the Leatherwood foothills we could see this wildly painted bluff, and when we looked out the front door of our cabin it loomed before us. My older sister Ellen told me—and I believed her—that there was nothing else in this world as beautiful as the Calico Rock.

Past the base of the Rock rushed the crystal-clear waters of White River, a spring-fed stream that winds through the Ozark hills and just below the Calico Rock swings in a great bend to the south. When we crossed the River in a boat we could see its bed clearly, even where the water was fifteen feet deep. Brown and white gravel, shells, and white sand sparkled on the bottom as if they were only two or three feet below the surface. The remarkable translucency of the water had led the Indians to call the River the Unica, meaning *white*, and the French to name it the Rivière Blanche.

In the 1860s and '70s this was a remote part of the country, many miles from telegraphs, railroads, and the great cities of the land—of

*Henry R. Schoolcraft, *Schoolcraft in the Ozarks: Reprint of Journal of a Tour into the Interior of Missouri and Arkansas in 1818 and 1819*. Ed. Hugh Park (Van Buren, Arkansas: Press-Argus Printers, 1955), pp. 151-2.

which we knew so little that they did not seem real to us. Our one link with civilization was the steamboats, and these grand, mysterious travelers from a strange land far away let us know dimly that a world different from our own really did exist. In the 1860s traffic on the upper River was just reviving after the War but was increasing with every passing year. Most of the boats were modest in size and furnishings. Occasionally, however, during the high water season, the great boats from the Mississippi, "floating palaces" they were called, steamed up the White for brief visits, and we were dazzled by their size and beauty. When the musical tones of the whistle announced the approach of a steamboat, Ellen and I would run to the bank of the River two hundred yards from our cabin to see her when she first hove into view. And what a breathtaking sight she was, gleaming white against the blue Ozark hills, her exhaust pipes puffing great jets of white vapor, and her twin smokestacks pouring forth gorgeous smoke as black as night. Speechless, we would watch her grow larger until she slowly, ever so slowly, crept by the great Rock, which made her look like a toy boat, and finally vanished from sight up the River. For two small children growing up in a part of the country where the manner of living was primitive this was an unbelievable glimpse of another world.

These early fascinations, the Rock and the River, have proved to be lasting. I have never been able to leave the towering bluffs and the blue-clear streams of the White River country. And it is no accident that my first important job was clerk on the Steamer *Home*, a packet running the trade on the upper White River in the 1880s.

As I was born in 1864 I do not recall any of the hardships of the Civil War. During my boyhood, however, stories about the War were on the tongue of everyone in the hills, and I listened to some of them over and over. I heard tales of battles and camps and prisons, and even more often stories about the experiences of the people back home. The Leatherwoods were so far away from the military campaigns that the home folks knew little about the course of the War. When hostilities ended, there was little mourning over the "lost cause," and the few slaves who were freed on the farms in the river bottoms did not create any problems. But let no one think that our people did not share fully in the hardships that fell upon the rest of the South.

A good many of the people, probably most of them, had opposed secession, yet when war came the majority sympathized with the Confederates, and soon or late almost all of the able-bodied men enlisted in the army. With most of the men gone, the women, the older children, and the old men had to provide for themselves and the younger children. The struggles of the women were nothing short of heroic. They had to act as heads of their households, and as doctors. They had to be their own apothecaries and make all their medicines, for even though there might be a little money hidden somewhere about the house, no drugs could be bought. They had to plant and plow the crops, such as they were. In the later years of the war the work had to be done by hand, for the horses and mules had been carried away by soldiers and bushwhackers.

Once a crop had been planted, the problems of the women had only begun. Time and again the young corn and vegetables were trampled under foot by soldiers and bushwhackers. If it was not ruined or stolen before harvest time, it was likely to be, later on. The housewife looked upon soldiers, even Confederates, as enemies, because they threatened death to her family and herself by starvation. Every family pooled their wits in deciding upon the best place to hide their food. Sometimes it was buried in the ground or hidden in hollow logs, trees, or caves; sometimes concealed in walls, floors, or rock piles. Women did not confide in one another about their hiding places. In spite of all precautions, however, the food was often found and carried away. In the first year and a half of the War small bands of Confederates came through the country and raided the smoke-houses, where the men had stored supplies of meat before taking up arms, and carried away all surplus horses and mules along with the food. The pillage was worse when the Federals came through. But the climax of woe was reached when the bushwhackers or jayhawkers made their raids. The regulars usually left something, but the bush-whackers never hesitated to take anything they wanted.

From the many stories of pillage and murder which circulated during my early years, I cite a few told by T. J. Estes, who in 1861-65 was a boy living in a neighboring county. When the Federals came to Yellville in the winter of 1864-65, they captured a young man named William Bassett and kept him a prisoner in the south room of the Estes house. Soon young Estes missed him and a day or two later found him at the edge of the woods, shot dead and stripped of most of his clothing. The third day after he was killed, Tom Jobe was shot. The Federals buried him in a shallow grave that was scratched into by dogs or wolves. Then the men went to where Bassett still lay un-buried and after digging a shallow grave, took him by the arms and dragged him to it, threw him in, punched his arms down with spades, and covered him with curses and a few inches of earth. One night while Estes was sitting on his porch he saw the blaze of pistols that ended the life of old man Elzy, who was shot for his money by a jawhawker. Some of the bushwhackers hanged Uncle Daniel Wickersham until nearly dead in order to get his money—and did get five hundred dollars—then shot and killed him. The same gang also killed Uncle Carroll Whitlock, a very poor and inoffensive man, for no cause whatever except that they liked to see people die. One night Webb's company of bushwhackers came into town after the Federals left and burned thirty-two houses. Two of them came into the Estes house, took fire out of the fireplace on a shovel and told Estes' mother they would burn her house if she did not tell them where her husband's money was hidden. But she shamed and demeaned them, so they merely pilfered her house and burned other buildings. Some old men's feet were baked to a crisp before hot fires and sometimes their toe nails were pulled out to make them tell where the valuables were. Estes' well-known stories show that when the Ozark area lost the protection that the pioneer men offered, the frontier reverted to savagery.

The full story of the bushwhackers or jayhawkers has never been and never will be told—for the reason that I will not tell all that I know of them. These freebooters were not soldiers. They were neighbors, geographically, of those they robbed and killed, but were anything but neighbors morally. Actually they were organized bands of thieves and murderers who made periodic raids on the women and children and old men and stole their cattle and their meager supplies of food and feed. When the War ended, some of the children of these outlaws remained in the hills and became good citizens. The people who had known their fathers talked freely and bitterly about the jayhawker bands, but few were willing to put any names in print. This was the case in the Leatherwoods, and since I know and respect the descendants of the leading jayhawker of our neighborhood, I will not give his name.

With a dozen or more followers A—— operated out of a locality near the present village of Lone Rock and terrorized the area from the mouth of the Buffalo River down the White to Sylamore. Between these two points every settlement and every household was at the mercy of these unprincipled men. A—— knew all the settlers along the River and in the hills nearby and, whenever he chose, he raided them, ransacking house and barn, carrying away whatever he and his band could use, ofttimes taking the last horse, mule, cow, or sheep,

the last bushel of corn or meal, and the last middling* of meat from homes where little children were living on half rations. Occasionally runners rushed through a neighborhood ahead of A—— and warned the villagers and farmers of the coming raid, and if the man of the house happened to be at home on furlough and if he was prudent, he might take to the woods and hide away lest the raiders kill him. In all cases the housewives would beg and plead with the jayhawkers, but A—— did not listen to their pleas.

The work animals of my own parents dwindled from half a dozen down to one mule. In 1864 my father was given a short furlough so that he might come home and plant a crop. While he was plowing in the fields, A——, his erstwhile neighbor, rode up at the head of a dozen of his kind and said, "Bob, I've got to have that mule." My father's heart sank at the thought of giving up the only work animal on the place, and he pleaded, for the sake of his wife and children, to be left with the mule, at least until he could plow his land, but without effect. He had to stand by and see his mule taken from the plow and carried away, along with other booty.

My uncle, William Swan, was more fortunate than my father in providing for his family. He was kept out of the army by a lame leg, and being on his place all the time, he used his energy and wits to raise a crop and then to see that enough was hidden away to take care of his household. By a clever strategem he saved his last work animal, a mare named Dough. With his knife he ripped long gashes on either side of her backbone, so that she could not be ridden. It was a cruel thing to do, but when A——'s band came and found her back in such condition, they swore a few oaths and went on, leaving old Dough behind. When the wounds began to heal, Uncle ripped them open again. These surgical operations, sorrowfully performed upon the mare, saved her for his own use.

Eventually A—— and his band were destroyed. In fact they were making their last raid when they took my father's mule. Several Confederates were on furlough at the same time as my father, and word went up and down the river that the jayhawkers were raiding. A band of volunteers was quickly formed and went in search of A——. One of his gang named Hedgpeth crossed the river and took a cow and calf from Mrs. Cynthia Shipp Wolf. As the calf was too young to walk, he carried it away on his horse. When word of this raid reached

*The middle or side of a hog between the ham and the shoulder; the part that is made into bacon.

a relative of mine, he immediately cut across a hill ahead of Hedg-peth, and when he saw the jayhawker coming down the trail driving the cow with the calf across his saddle, he drew a bead on the thief and shot him off his horse, dead. The cow and calf were taken back to the owner, and my kinsman joined the posse.

The following morning the posse was in close pursuit of A——'s band, who were feeling perfectly safe, riding slowly north-ward along the River road, slowed down by the livestock they had stolen. A Negro, old Gumbo, was bringing up the rear on my father's mule, driving a slow-footed yoke of oxen, which had been stolen from a neighbor of ours. The posse left Gumbo behind and hurried on to overtake A—— and his band. Two miles above Shipp's Ferry they rode suddenly upon the jayhawkers, and took them wholly unawares. The shooting began at once and two or three of the raiders were killed. They had no time to organize for defense, but fled from the river road to the woods. Hard-pressed, A—— undertook to escape by climbing the hill that rose from the roadside. He was quickly recognized and singled out for a target. Dodging behind trees, he shot at his pursuers sixteen times, but never hit one. Slowly he retreated up the hill until he was close to the ledge at the top, where he took hold of a grapevine that hung over the top, so as to climb the few remaining feet to safety—at least temporary safety. But in so doing he exposed himself to the guns of the posse, and one of the number, Tom Speers, settled on one knee, rested an elbow on the other knee, took careful aim with his long-barreled rifle, and fired. A—— relaxed his hold on the vine and tumbled half-way down the bluff. Speers turned to Hardin C. Shipp and exclaimed, "Hard, I got him that time!"

The men rushed up the hill to where A—— lay cursing and trying to shoot, but he was too weak. His pistols were wrenched from his hands, and a man named Keeling quickly pulled off his boots. In explanation Keeling said, "The damned thief swore that he would die with his boots on; I'm going to see that he dies with them off." Eleven of the jayhawkers were killed on that same day, and the gang was virtually wiped out.

When the posse regrouped they drove the stolen horses and cattle, including my father's mule, back down the trail and delivered them to their owners. As nearly every able-bodied man in the com-munity was in the posse, my father and my uncle may have been members—I never heard them say. So ended the depredations of A——'s band of jayhawkers.

During the following years several long-barreled rifles were exhibited in Baxter and Izard Counties, each certified to be the one that killed A——. It is quite possible that other men besides Speers hit A—— as he swung on the grapevine or tumbled down the hill, so that there may have been more than one rifle that deserved the claims made for it, though hardly as many as were said to have ended the life of the notorious jayhawker.

My mother and my sister lived during the winters of the War period mainly on hoecakes and sweet milk. One or two cows in the neighborhood had been saved from the marauders by being driven into the woods to forage during the day, since the raids in the Leatherwoods never came at night. When spring arrived and the early wild herbs and other growth began to sprout, my mother would have the children of the neighborhood follow the cows through the woods and gather the kinds of greens that the cows ate; cows will not eat poisonous plants. A few years later, after the death of my father, hard times came upon our family again, and I was one of the children that followed the cows as they grazed. In doing so, I learned that old field lettuce, burdock, poke, lamb's quarter, tongue grass, deer's tongue, dandelion, sheep sorrel, and some other plants are nonpoisonous and when cooked like mustard greens are palatable if one is hungry. I remember that we had many a mess of this kind of greens. Other families in our area lived during the hardest years of the War on tree bark and wild grass and weeds.

As in other parts of the South during the War years, the need for salt was desperate and was met by using the floor dirt from the smokehouses. In the winters of past years when hogs were killed, the hams, shoulders, and sides were salted and hung from smokehouse rafters to cure. For about three weeks salty grease oozed out of the meat and dripped to the dirt floor, making large spots that through the years became saturated with salt. When families grew desperate for salt during the War, they dug up the dirt from the smokehouse floors and put it into hoppers. Water was poured on and the salt dissolved in the water, which was strained and finally boiled down to salt. It was brown in color, but it served the purpose very well.

The last winter of 1864-65, which Aunt Eliza Swan always called "the year of the famine," almost finished some of the people in the upper White River country. The jayhawkers were no longer a threat, but the rest of our troubles were growing more acute. More than one family that I heard of lived for days on the tender part of tree bark cooked in fireplaces. A Mr. B—— killed a skunk and buried it, but several days later he grew desperate for food, dug up the animal, and ate it. He said that it was the sweetest meat he had ever tasted.

During this "year of the famine," the Swans fed themselves and their children on hoecakes. Uncle made a careful check on his corn and reckoned that he had enough to carry his family through the winter, with probably a little over. Once a month he took a bushel of corn from his hidden supply to Benbrook's mill across the river seven miles away. The women and children living along the trail which led to the mill would see him riding by with his sack and would lie in wait for him on his return trip, to beg him for a little meal. The stories they would tell him of privation and suffering, and the starvation that showed in their faces were too much for his rugged heart, and he would dole out his meal, here a little, there a little—the meal which meant so much to his own household—until by the time he reached home he would have given away half his grist.

Aunt was puzzled by the meager supply he brought home, and plied him with sharp questions until he confessed that on his trips from the mill he had been giving away the meal to their neediest neighbors. My aunt, who prided herself on being a bit hard when the situation justified, had taken note of the dwindling supply of corn in their hide-away and now foresaw how it was all going to end—this generosity of Mr. Swan's. She berated him stoutly, told him he was robbing the orphan children they had taken to raise, and he promised to do better thereafter. Before he left on his next trip to the mill, Aunt gave him another sharp warning. He listened in patience, repeated his promises, saddled his mare, laid the sack of corn across the front of the saddle, and rode away. When he returned, the half-limp sack of meal told Aunt the same story of his misplaced generosity, and she scolded him mightily. The next time they needed meal she would go herself, she said, and she vowed she would bring home a full sack. She went.

On the way back from the mill a woman stopped her and begged her for a little meal. Her husband was in the army. She had four children at home, all weak with hunger. They were entirely out of food. They had not had anything to eat that day, and she could not bear to hear her children crying for bread. Wouldn't Mrs. Swan, please, for God's sake, give her a little meal—just a quart—please, please! The sack was opened and the meal was given. She was next met at the fork of the road by a little girl who lifted her thin arms in entreaty. Her mother was sick in bed right over yonder in that house. They had not had anything to eat except a cup of milk since yesterday morning, and were so hungry. Wouldn't Mrs. Swan please give them some meal—just a little—and when their father came home from the army he would pay for it. Aunt shared with them some of her meal. Farther on, she was met by an old man, by other women and children whose sunken cheeks and hollow eyes told their story more forcefully than words could have done. When she reached home her sack of meal was almost empty. And that, she said, was her last trip to the mill.

After Uncle died and Aunt came to live in my home in Batesville, where she spent the last years of her long life, she was often called upon at dinner parties and other small social gatherings to tell the story of her trip to the mill, and she did a masterly job of it. Since her twentieth year the fingers of her left hand had been drawn up and permanently frozen in that position. In telling a story she gesticulated freely, using most effectively her crippled hand—erysipelas hand, she called it. I can see her today telling this story in her quick sharp phrases and accenting her words with her thin arms and hands, the left in particular, and I can see her listeners motionless in attention.

When the War was over and the surviving men returned to the hills, troubles were soon ended—but not, of course, in those families bereft of husband and father. Since we lived independently of the rest of the world in times of peace, Reconstruction meant to us clearing farms of briars, rebuilding the ruined fences, and making a garden. As soon as the farmers in the Leatherwoods were able to clear their fields and make one or two good crops, trade for a cow or two and three or four hogs, life returned to its old ways.

Chapter II
On the Banks of the White River

The happy days on the banks of the White were not to last long. When I was in my sixth year my father died, and during the next few years our family was not a very cheerful one. My mother was deep in grief and seemed uncertain about how to plan for herself and her children. She rented our good farm in the bottoms and we moved across the River so as to be near a school.

I recall one trivial incident that occurred when we were on the way to our new home. We went by ox wagon, and as we were crossing the River at Talbert's Ferry, a half dozen or so cattle on the boat became excited and, in spite of the efforts of the ferryman to quiet them, one of them jumped overboard and struck out straight down the River. The ferryman yelled out, "Go to hell, you Campbellite," whereupon everyone laughed lustily—everyone except me: I had no idea what a Campbellite* was. Our new cabin home was small, and our meals were slender during the ensuing winter. We did not see many biscuits, even on Sundays. There were no cookstoves in our neighborhood, and all cooking was done in the fireplace. I remember watching Mother prepare our meals: she would bake three corn dodgers in a skillet over a shovelful of live coals on the hearth, would put a lid on the skillet and live coals on the lid to equalize the heat so that

*"Campbellite" was a derogatory term for a follower of Alexander Campbell, founder of the Disciples of Christ, who emphasize the saving power of baptism by immersion. A story similar to Wolf's is quoted by Mitford Mathews (*Dictionary of Americanisms*, I, 252) from *Harper's Magazine* of July 1872. A small boy, on being asked why he calls crappie "Campbellites," replies, "Because they spoil so quick after I get them out of the water."

the bread would cook uniformly. With the corn dodgers we had sweet milk to drink—and that was our fare—not very elaborate but wholesome enough, and we lived on it the entire winter of 1871-72.

For two growing children, however, the clouds did not hang very low. Four miles from us lived my aunt and uncle, Mr. and Mrs. William T. Swan, whose home was cheerful and pleasant. I had spent a Christmas with them and remembered well the good things we had to eat—apples and biscuits and honey and butter, jams and jellies and pear preserves, pies and cakes. This visit held a prominent place in my memory, and the following summer I persuaded my mother to let me pay the Swans a drop-in visit. I was glad to find that the food at the Swans' was still as good and as plentiful as before, but I made a discovery of something even more interesting to me than good things to eat—a chest filled with back numbers of the *American Agriculturist*, published by Orange, Judd and Company somewhere in the East. These magazines were filled with woodcuts of fine horses, cattle, sheep, goats, hogs, chickens, ducks, and geese. They were the first picture-books I had seen, and the woodcuts were so wonderful to me that to look at them for three hours, three blissful hours, was ample reward for my eight-mile walk, which I repeated during the summer as often as I was allowed to go. If I could have seen one of today's picture magazines, I believe I would have burst with excitement.

When I was eight, Mr. William Hixson, a neighbor living two miles away, made a week-long trip to Missouri, and Mrs. Hixson asked that I stay at her home to help with the live stock during her husband's absence. On my first day there she handed me the most marvelous book that I had ever feasted my eyes upon. Never before had I seen a book with colored pictures. It was *Mother Goose Melodies*, with unbelievably comical and attractive illustrations. During the next few days I pored over its pages and read over and over again every one of its jolly jingles until I knew by heart "Old King Cole," "Jack Be Nimble," "Mother Hubbard," and all the rest from start to finish. In fact, I was so carried away with this literary find that to this day I have not forgotten those merry nursery rimes or those bright-colored pictures.

Nor can I forget the time one January during a bitterly cold spell my mother had a neighbor "snake up" six long hickory trees for us to use as firewood. We had the proverbial widow woman's dull axe for cutting up the trees into the right length for the fireplace, and the job of doing the chopping fell to my sister and me. It took us children all day to cut enough wood to last until the next day. One of us would go out and cut for half an hour while the other sat by the fire. Then we would exchange places.

On a day when the weather was unusually raw and windy and cold, my sister came out to relieve me about four o'clock in the afternoon. She stayed out a long time, but I was not curious to learn why, since the axe-strokes were falling regularly, and I felt that my time would come soon enough. When I had taken my last turn three long saplings with all the limbs snaked off remained to be chopped up. Presently my sister bounded in, her face beaming, and announced that she had finished up all the wood. The news was so incredible that I ran outside to see if it was true. Sure enough, there lay the wood all cut up into fire-place length, from foresticks and go-between sticks to biggest logs. I ran back into the house to say that Ellen's story was true. My mother knew that it was an impossible feat and asked Ellen for an explanation. The truth came out. Passing our way, Mr. James Hamilton had seen the little girl hacking away with a dull axe at the hickory trees, dismounted from his horse, hitched his horse to the gatepost, whetted the axe with a sandstone, and chopped up the trees. He had then got on his horse and ridden away. We saw tears running down Mother's face as she explained that Mr. Hamilton and our father had belonged to the same lodge.

You may imagine what a deep impression this act made on me. Here was a man, some miles from home, late in this cold winter day, with a river to cross, who took the time to do a deed of genuine charity, and then rode away without saying a word about it. I wonder if such helpfulness exists today among the members of fraternal organizations.

Another memorable character was our postmaster. I looked upon him as one of the really big men of our neighborhood—a person of eminence and distinction. Mail came to our post office every Saturday with clocklike regularity—provided that the River was not too high, or the mud not too deep, or the weather not too cold, or the carrier not feeling bad. About the only mail our household ever got was the *Farm and Home* magazine, which came once a month, but some one of us always went to the post office on Saturdays. If the someone was Walton, who lived with Ellen and me at the Swan's after our mother's death, or I or both of us, we loitered about to watch the postmaster at work and to see the people get their mail. The office had one pigeon-hole for letters and one for all other mail. I was deeply impressed by our dignified, business-like postmaster and realized how high he must stand in the business of the federal government.

His professional manner as he ran through the mail, tossing a letter to this person and that, was efficiency of the highest degree.

One Monday when I was on some other errand than inquiring for the mail, I saw the postmaster working in his garden and leaned on his fence to admire him. Several people who had not come for mail on Saturday did so on this Monday, and then and there I received evidence of the postmaster's remarkable memory that elicited my warmest admiration. At intervals these neighbors walked up to the garden fence and asked for mail. With only a glance and without a moment's hesitation he replied, "You didn't get no mail." What a memory he had! Unfortunately, however, I was to be disillusioned. On a Monday following the Saturday when our *Farm and Home* always came, I found our postmaster looking at his growing corn and told him I had come for our mail. Instantly he answered, "You didn't get none." I knew quite well that *Farm and Home* was in the box and by rapid mental calculation concluded that although his memory might be excellent and his disinclination to unnecessary effort well-developed, his veracity was affected by circumstances and sometimes took a holiday.

Thus did one of my boyhood heroes topple from his high perch.

When I was five years old I attended the Masonic funeral of Robert Livingston, a pioneer settler who came into Izard County in 1820. It was conducted in the upper room of a house on the River. A short fat man stood at the foot of the outside stairway which led up to a room on the second floor. He wore white gloves and a short white apron and carried a shiny sword in his right hand. I had never before seen anyone dressed in this way. Several men in gloves and aprons went up the stairs without being challenged by the fat man with the sword, while other men in ordinary clothes stood around in the yard showing no inclination to go near to the stairway. I did not understand, and I asked who the men were who were wearing aprons. I was told that they were Masons and that the fat man with the sword was a guard placed at the stairs to keep anyone who was not a Mason from going up. It looked like a dangerous situation to me, and I moved back about forty feet. I had no doubt that if anybody, big or little, male or female, other than a Mason, should attempt to go up the stairway, the fat guard would sever his head from his body with one swing. It seemed like a miracle to me that nobody's head was cut off that day, and I went home with pictures of swords and fat swordsmen spinning in my head.

Of course, the main concern of these early years was school.

There were no free schools in the Leatherwoods—only subscription schools, almost always taught by men. Today people would be surprised and probably amused by some of the features of our back-woods schools. First of all, our buildings never had more than one room, and they were well filled with young people of ages from five to twenty. The rooms had dirt floors and split-log seats with no backs and with rough hickory pegs for legs. A second difference from the schools of today was that during study periods the pupils were required to study aloud—and we made quite a hubbub, with each of us reading or spelling or figuring from a different book or page. Of course, we were taught only the three R's and spelling. The spelling bees were the high point of our instruction and were considered so important that "the public" was invited to attend them on Fridays; some people drove for miles to watch these "battles," as they were called. Still another difference was that no one ever spoke of being in a certain grade—because the schools were not graded—but of being in a certain reader or arithmetic, McGuffey's Third, for example. There was good horse-sense in the ungraded school, since it was always geared to a student's strong and weak points. For instance, he could be in the fifth reader and the second arithmetic at the same time.

Before my father's death Ellen, who was three years older than I, attended a term of school at the village of Calico Rock, making the trip across the River in a canoe, and sometimes I went with her, though I was only four. On these visits I always wore a one-piece dress-like garment—nothing else. There wasn't much to it—in fact, its length was hardly worth mentioning. My sister taught me a speech, and on a Friday I said it for the school—still in my one-piece attire. It brought down the house—the attire, not the speech; but what a cold and critical world thought about my outfit mattered little to me. The only other event of this pre-school session that I recall is that one of the pupils, John Mackey, died and the whole school marched to the graveyard, two and two, a boy and a girl. I had to march the two-mile round trip with a six-year old girl, Mollie Dillard, and I felt so humiliated and abused that I sulked and refused to say a word, going or coming.

At the end of that year the Calico Rock school closed and we moved to Lead Hill, where Ellen and I attended Mr. Wofford's school. The one-room house loomed in my mind as a large building, long and tall and wide, and the creek bank where it stood seemed like the precipitous bank of a river. Years later I revisited the spot and found the whole place shrunken—the schoolhouse a mere box and the schoolhouse creek a small spring branch with five-foot banks. At this school I learned my ABC's, learned to spell words of one syllable, and, I suppose, made my way through McGuffey's First, though I have no recollection of learning to read. Much more clearly I remember my behavior problems. I was not used to boys, because I had none as brothers or as neighbors, and I found that they were hilariously funny. As a result their antics made me laugh out loud. If one of them made a paper wad and thumped it at another, I guffawed; if he made an ugly face at the teacher behind his back, I exploded; if he stuck a pin in someone, I whooped. After these outbursts I always had to go up to the front of the room to be whipped—on an average of twice a day. Since the boys enjoyed my hearty responses to their showing off and were entertained by my punishments, they always made sure I was watching when they misbehaved. Like all other boys and girls I was barefoot, and Mr. Wofford whipped me with a reed or a green cane on my feet. I would hop about like a country dancer, though my antics were without grace and rhythm. I remember getting whipped six times in one day. But, oh, it was funny—seeing the boys shoot those paper wads.

Another boy in the school, Robert McManus, was afflicted with the same weakness of laughing out loud, and I cannot say which of us was whipped oftener. One Friday just before closing time we both guffawed, and the teacher, being tired and eager to go home, postponed our whipping until Monday morning. As soon as school opened on Monday he called for us two six-year-olds, and I arose promptly and walked up the aisle. When I had almost reached the platform, I heard a scraping noise on the floor behind me, and suddenly the room broke out in laughter. I looked around to see what the cause was, and there was McManus shuffling up the aisle dragging a pair of ancient brogan shoes, about size twelve. He had tied them with heavy twine so as to protect his feet, probably still sore from last week's whippings. Teacher and pupils alike joined in the laughter, and I have an idea that his strategy lightened the licking that we got on that Monday morning.

The best of my school days were spent under Dr. J. A. Kerr of Newburgh, Arkansas, an attractive young man with curly red hair, who taught very successful terms at Spring Creek during the years 1875, '76, and '77. His school attracted a good deal of attention and drew patronage from miles around. In 1875 we were living in Calico Rock, a small community on the top of the big bluff with the same name, and Ellen and I walked three and a half miles to and from

Spring Creek every morning and afternoon. The schoolhouse stood in a grove of big trees beside a small mountain creek surrounded by the unspoiled Ozark hills. A hundred yards from the building a fine everlasting spring gushed out from under a hill.

Like most schoolmasters of the day in frontier communities, Dr. Kerr maintained strict discipline by means of the switch. One Friday two of the big boys in the school, Jim Alex Staggs and Charlie Cantrell, both from prominent families in the neighborhood, had a fight on the school grounds, and Dr. Kerr announced just before dismissal that they would be whipped when school opened Monday morning. After school hours Jim Alex told some of his friends that he would not take the whipping, and the community spent the weekend speculating on what might happen on Monday. When school opened, both boys were in their places, with members of their families occupying seats on the stage, and a large number of visitors were present, including the trustees of the school. Most of the visitors appeared to be worried, but a few bristled as though they expected and hoped for a fight.

Dr. Kerr walked onto the stage, carrying two long, rough ironwood switches, and he looked pale but determined as he called on the two young men to come forward and take their punishment. Cantrell arose promptly and walked up to the edge of the two-foot-high platform. He wore a suit of medium-heavy homespun jeans. Dr. Kerr stepped forward on the platform and gave Charlie nine licks, whipping him downward over the left shoulder and putting all his strength into every stroke. Two of the lashes cut three-inch slits in Charlie's pants. The boy swerved a little as each stroke fell, but he made no outcry, not even a whimper. After the ninth lick Dr. Kerr told him to take his seat, which he did.

Dr. Kerr then called on Jim Alex to come forward for his whipping. The boy arose promptly and said defiantly, "I will not take it," whereupon Dr. Kerr announced that he was expelled from the school. In a second everyone on the stage was on his feet shouting protests and threats. I suppose that some of the visitors had planned a demonstration or fight, but finding the odds against them, changed their minds. There was, however, some minor scuffling. Elijah Cantrell seized a slate with both hands and threatened to break it over Joe Bell Staggs' head. But someone jumped between them and the blow was not delivered. The visitors milled about for a few minutes, and all the girls and women rushed from the building. But Dr. Kerr loudly commanded everyone to be seated and then made a short speech which restored order. When he felt sure that the danger of violence had passed, he called a recess. Charlie Cantrell's friends quickly gathered around him and congratulated him for his grit in taking a severe whipping rather than being expelled from the school. Jim Alex and his friends withdrew without creating further disturbance. This was the only serious trouble during Dr. Kerr's three terms at Spring Creek, an unusual record for those days when teachers were often beaten and driven from their schools.

Under Dr. Kerr I became firmly grounded in the three R's and in spelling. At the end of the third term I had almost finished McGuffey's fifth reader and Ray's third part arithmetic and had been through the Blue-Back Speller eleven times—could spell every word in it. A number of good spellers were developed at this Spring Creek school, among them Dan Hively, Emma Wood, and my sister Ellen. Spelling was the popular branch of study at Dr. Kerr's school, largely because of the Friday "battles" attended by the public. In fact, both school and visitors looked forward eagerly to these weekly bees as a popular pastime. On the last day of the second term I attended the school held a battle which drew more than the usual number of visitors, and Ellen and I were named to choose up sides. The spelling began at one p.m.; Dr. Kerr "gave out" until he gave out and turned the book over to a visitor. After an hour he too was tired, and a third pronouncer took over. When eventually Dr. Kerr resumed the job everyone on both sides had long since been eliminated except Ellen and me. We stood up until sundown, page after page and hour after hour, and neither of us missed a word, so Dr. Kerr had to declare the battle a draw. This was the first time I had been able to stand up to Ellen, and I was quite chesty about it.

In the everyday spelling classes (different from the Friday afternoon bees) we stood in a single long row and "turned down" those who stumbled over words that we could spell. During my first session at Spring Creek, when I was somewhere near the middle of the row of spellers, the word *wren* was given out to the pupil standing at the head of the class. He missed, spelling it *r-e-n*; the second in line tried *r-e-n-n*; the third, *r-i-n*. By the time a half dozen pupils had missed, all the combinations that I could think of had been used and my mind was blank. But just below me stood Bob Benbrook, and luckily for me he knew the word. As spellers fell by the wayside, he became so excited and so afraid he would forget before it got to him that he couldn't hold the word in any longer and began to huff to himself, "w-r-e-n, w-r-e-n, w-r-e-n." I overheard and joyfully

pounced on the correct spelling, which I eagerly delivered to the teacher and walked to the head of the class with an air of importance and superiority which plainly said, "See what a fellow can do who knows how." I never had the courage to tell Benbrook how I snatched that head-mark out of his mouth.

During my last term of school at Spring Creek Dan Hively was at the head of the class and stayed there for five weeks. I worked my way up to him but there I stalled, for Dan was a good speller. By the rule of practice in that day everybody kept his position in the spelling row unless he missed a word and was turned down or was absent from school. It seemed to me that I would never get to the head of the class. But one Friday Dan did not come to school, and in accordance with the rules he had to go to the foot on Monday, and I stepped into his shoes at the head—the place I had been longing to occupy for five long weeks. When the spelling class started Monday it looked good to see Dan so far away down at the foot and to find myself in the long-coveted place as head of the line. I profoundly hoped that it would take him a long time to work back up near me. But my hopes were blasted when the teacher gave out the word *precipice* to the pupil next to me. I was uneasy when he missed it, for the good spellers were always near the head, but I comforted myself with the thought that the word had to run the gamut of a dozen good spellers and two dozen others before Hively would get a chance at it. But somehow the good spellers stumbled and fell. I stepped forward two steps where I could get a good look at the entire row and immediately concluded with sinking heart that not one of them except Hively could spell the word correctly. About a third of the way down the line stood Mollie Pearson, a girl about thirteen who was a fairly good speller. Evidently most of the combinations of letters that she could think of had been tried and proved wrong so she offered a new one. I will never forget the saline flavor she gave to the last syllable of the word, which set the whole school by the ears—everyone had a good laugh. The word went on down, just as I predicted to myself, until it got to Dan, who pounced on it like a hungry cat on a piece of beef liver and came walking the whole length of the thirty-five or forty members of the class, right next to me, to be a constant thorn in my side. But happy to relate, he never went ahead of me, and I held my place until the end of the session.

My school days at Spring Creek were brought to a sudden end by the death of my mother when I was twelve. Ellen and I went in a two-horse wagon to the graveyard at the mouth of Moccasin Creek.

When the lid of the coffin was removed, I saw drops of perspiration all over Mother's forehead, and I heard people at the graveside question whether she was really dead or in a state of suspended animation. The burial proceeded, however, and she was duly interred beside my father and four of her children. In later days I attended a few more terms of school, but none so memorable as those under Dr. Kerr at Spring Creek.

Chapter III
The Abundant Life in a Log Cabin

Upon the death of my mother, Ellen and I were taken to the home of my father's sister and her husband, Mr. and Mrs. William T. Swan, who lived across the river back in the Leatherwood Hills four or five miles from the farm in the bottoms where I was born—and who had the woodcut magazines and the good things to eat. Under the circumstances the outlook for me could not have been brighter. Unlike almost all the other houses in the Leatherwoods, which were one-room log cabins, the Swan home had two good-sized rooms and a porch in the front the entire width of the house. There were no windows in either room, but each had two doors and a fireplace. The kitchen and the smoke-house were twenty-five feet removed from the cabin. Three hundred yards away a fine cold spring poured out of a limestone cave. The Swans were good, industrious people with a strong sense of responsibility for their children. Childless themselves, they raised first and last, at least thirteen and perhaps as many as sixteen orphans, about half of whom preceded Ellen and me. When we arrived we found two children already living there, Annie Wolf, our cousin, and Willie Walton, a nine-year-old. In May 1863 word came to Agnes Wolf, wife of my Uncle Mike Wolf, that her sister, who lived several miles away at Big Flat, was dangerously ill. She took her thirteen-month-old child, Annie, and left on horseback to go to her sister, accompanied by a boy on foot. Near the river her horse stumbled and threw her against a stump. Realizing that she was badly injured she had the boy cross the river for help, placing the uninjured baby as close to her as possible. When help arrived Agnes was dead and the baby was playing in the water at the river's edge.

Uncle Mike gave the baby Annie and an older child to his sister, Mrs. Eliza Swan, to care for. Annie was fourteen and had been living with the Swans for thirteen years when Ellen and I went to live there. Willie's father had sent for the Swans four years earlier when he was dying of tuberculosis and had begged them to let him give them his five-year-old son as their own. They had accepted the boy unconditionally, and when Mr. Walton died a few months later, they took Willie to their home in the Leatherwoods several miles away. As long as I knew them, Mr. Swan was a real father to Willie, and Willie in turn gave my uncle the loyalty and devotion of a true son.

Mr. Swan had come to Arkansas from Bastrop, Louisiana, before the Civil War, and in 1852 had married my aunt Eliza, the oldest daughter of the Reverend John Wolf, a pioneer preacher who died while serving as a chaplain in the War. Mr. Swan had first farmed in the rich River bottoms, but as it was generally believed that the damp air near the River was injurious to health, he had moved into the Leatherwood Hills. There was a great difference between the low, fertile fields of Louisiana and the rocky lands and poor soil of the Leatherwoods. What Mr. Swan may have known about farming in Louisiana was not worth much to him in the hills of North Arkansas. But he used common sense in farm management and quickly learned by experience what kind of crops his land would produce and what to plant in the different soils of his farm. He rotated his crops and never made a total failure. His oats might fail, but his millet would be good; his late corn might be caught by the drouth, but his early corn would make a good yield. Likewise with his clover, his cow peas, his cotton, his wheat. He had an excellent orchard of more than ₋ hundred trees which did not need spraying, a strawberry patch, and a row of raspberry bushes. His wife and the two girls were busy all summer canning, preserving, making jam and jelly, drying apples and peaches on scaffolds and roofs. About a dozen hives of bees were on the place, and we had honey on the table at every meal in the year. To provide vegetables for winter use, we dug two or three holes in the garden about four feet deep, lined them with straw, and used them to store cabbages, lettuce, turnips, potatoes, and beets (also apples). In January when we went into the holes, we found the fruit and vegetables almost as fresh as when we put them in. From six to ten cows provided all the milk, cream, and butter the family needed, with some left over for the hogs. Razorbacks had the run of the woods most of the year and got fat on mast. Late in the fall we penned them and fed them corn to sweeten the meat, and when winter came we butchered eight to ten, which furnished an ample supply of ham, shoulders, middlings, sausage, and lard to run the family until the next hog-killing time. Very early Uncle saw the profit in raising cattle, for they ran on the free ranges all the year, finding abundant forage in the winter on the south sides of the hills, up the coves, and along the creeks and the river valleys where cane was abundant. Only in severe cold snaps were they brought in to be nubbined.* From October to March we butchered and ate a few beeves. In the spring Uncle sold from ten to twenty-five head of cattle to Missouri buyers and in the fall two or three bales of cotton, which brought in more than enough money for the family needs. So far as I know, he never bought a bushel of corn or borrowed a dollar in his life.

When I first came to Uncle's he had only a yoke of oxen and two plows, a turning and a bull-tongue, to make his crops. With the turning plow he broke up the ground for planting, and later, as the cotton and corn grew, he stirred the soil and threw fresh earth up to the plants. With the bull-tongue he plowed out the middles. A few months later he traded for a span of horses and a wagon, and in another year or two he bought a double-shovel plow, which cut his work in half. During the first two years we used the old-fashioned eye hoes with pawpaw handles, heavy and unwieldy. If the soil was heavy they accumulated dirt and weeds under the eye and grew even heavier and more tiring. When we got goose-neck hoes, I thought I had seen the mechanical wonder of the age.

Nearly every farmer had a tobacco patch, and when the tobacco leaves got "in case," that is, ready to handle without crumbling, he would shape them into twists for smoking or chewing. Uncle was one of the few farmers in the hills who raised wheat and who therefore provided his family with the luxury of biscuits for breakfast and supper. He cut the grain with an old-fashioned, backbreaking cradle (cradle-scythe) and threshed it in a treadmill powered by horses or mules working the alternate shifts, two at a time. These harvesting methods were crude and laborious, but they gave us biscuits —wonderful, heavenly biscuits. Methinks I see two tired and hungry boys sitting down to supper, splitting open their biscuits, laying them crumb-side down in black fried-ham gravy so they would soak it up like a sponge, and then making just four bites of each half of the split biscuit. Country biscuits are not small. The wheat and corn were ground by water mills, of which there were several in our area.

*That is, fed the dwarf or stunted ears of corn.

Thinking over the relative merits of water-mill biscuits and commercial-flour biscuits, I positively take my stand on the side of the water-mill variety. From this stand I will not be moved.

We slept in corded beds that sagged about a foot in the middle and made a more or less comfortable curve in the back of the sleeper. But deep, squashy feather mattresses kept us snug and gave us peaceful sleep.

A permanent home, hot biscuits, ham and black gravy, a feather bed—ah, this was the lap of luxury!

During my first two or three years at the Swans' we had no lamps, either brass or glass. Instead we used candles made in pewter candle-molds with a capacity of twelve. These gave illumination to cook and eat by, for let it be remembered that during the greater part of the year we ate breakfast before daybreak and supper after dark. Some of our neighbors used grease lamps, small iron or tin vessels filled two-thirds full of grease, with a twisted wick of coarse thread hanging over the edge of the vessel. The free end of the wick would dimly light a room. By and by we got a small round brass lamp with a round wick. Attached by a chain to the lamp was a small brass cap used to extinguish the light. This lamp was an improvement over the tallow candle and the grease lamp, but it was a poor light to read by. Rich pine knots thrown into the fireplace made a far better light for reading. A good-sized knot will light up a large room for fifteen minutes. Uncle finally bought a glass lamp with a glass chimney, perfection itself in artificial lighting.

There were no cook-stoves in the Leatherwoods until 1871. Meat and vegetables were cooked in pots set on the wood in the fireplace. The pots had to be balanced carefully to keep them from overturning when sticks of wood burned in two. Pies and other dishes were baked in the fireplace oven, and frying was done in skillets on the coals. In the course of time a neighbor, Dennis Dozier, became the agent for the Wrought Iron Range Company, of St. Louis, and sold Uncle a first-class range for $73 delivered, the first to break into the Leatherwoods. We used red cedar for stovewood.

Aunt Eliza looked the part of a pioneer housewife, tall and lean and strong, with weather-beaten face and hands. She gave us much better cooking than most of our neighbors enjoyed, and she kept our house clean. Once a month came "scouring days," when the furniture would be moved out and the floors thoroughly scrubbed with lye soap and white sand. A home-made mop was the scouring implement. Like most women in the Ozarks Aunt smoked a clay cane-stemmed pipe before and after breakfast, and after dinner and supper. She had an endless supply of stories and she told them well. Boy-like, I thought little about them, and today I can recall only a few —enough, however, to realize that she could have filled a volume with valuable folktales and historical yarns.

Uncle was not a strong man physically; he was slow-motioned, slow of speech, even-tempered, and the kindest, gentlest, most patient man I have ever known. His wants were few; his life was narrow and circumscribed. But in spite of these limitations he was a man of vision and foresight: he looked beyond his environment and his day. For example, the schools in the City Rock neighborhood where he lived were not good, and while his neighbors were content with these poor schools, he was not. He sent the orphan children who came under his care to better schools elsewhere. My sister and me he placed in the good academy at Mountain Home, which we attended for two years or four full terms; he sent Willie Walton to Pineville, where the school was considered thorough. Later he put him in medical college in Louisville, Kentucky, and for a special course in a school in Chicago. When I was twenty he made it possible for me to take a course in Bryant and Stratton's Business College in St. Louis.

The Swans were sane and well-anchored people; they had positive opinions, but were kind and tolerant. They had long since solved the problems of how to live in peace and comfort and plenty. No traveler through the hills who asked lodging for the night was ever turned away from their doors. No stranger or visitor who dropped in about mealtime but was fed. If there were needy people in the Leatherwoods—and at times there were a few—if there were families where misfortune had struck, the Swans came to their assistance without being called upon and gave as long as there was need. The fact that they raised so many orphan children shows better than words can do their sincere and generous love of people. In their home it was my happy lot to live during the formative years from twelve to twenty-one. Fortunate indeed was the orphan who fell into the hands of this couple.

Life in general was not eventful back in the hills where we four children were growing up. And our home at the Swans did not offer much for the entertainment of children, large or small. We had no toys and few books—only the chest full of back numbers of the *American Agriculturist,* a *Vinegar Bitters Almanac*, Dr. Gunn's *Domestic Medicine*, and the Holy Bible. We were a hundred miles from a railroad, and the so-called roads through the hills were very bad. Reaching our cabin by buggy was out of the question, and by wagon, difficult. Mail came to the post office a few miles away once a week, on Saturdays, but we expected little or none and were seldom disappointed. Fancy foods and fancy entertainments were unknown. I believe that twenty-five dollars would have taken care of all our cash needs for a year. We had to buy only coffee, salt, spices, sugar, rice, shoes, hats, nails, and horseshoes—even for some of these there were backwoods substitutes. Kentucky coffee-bean trees grew in the hills and from the beans a hot drink could be made that some of our neighbors liked; molasses (long sweetenin') sometimes took the place of sugar (I never saw white sugar until I went to the Swans'—we had used brown sugar, brought by boat up the River in hogsheads); and homespun headgear could be made by the women of the household. The blacksmith and the cobbler got a little of Uncle's cash. But we were by no means poor, as Uncle had more than enough money to pay for all necessities and to meet all emergencies. So with plenty to eat, soft featherbeds to sleep on, and not too much work to do, we were prosperous and contented.

If anyone supposes that in such a home and such a remote community, life must have been dull for Walton and me, he is very much mistaken. Our chores were not very heavy and part of them were welcome, such as feeding the livestock. More important, our minds were active, and something exciting was astir most of the time to keep them in motion. Life moved rapidly, and adventure was only as far away as the river or the woods, often even closer. Every day brought interesting experiences—at least they were interesting to us. It did not occur to us that anything was happening anywhere else in the world of much importance. We did not hear of foreign wars until they had ended, and they seemed as far away as the moon. We were busy discovering our own little world—and that was enough.

Life on an upland farm was quite a shocker to me. First of all, there was work to do. We got up at 4 a.m., and in the warm months we planted, plowed, hoed, chopped cotton, picked cotton. In the winter we cut wood, made fires, cleaned out fence corners, cleared land, shucked corn, fed the horses, often nubbined some thirty head of cattle, and gave corn to the hogs. We went to bed not long after dark.

An even greater shocker was my "brother," Willie Walton. He was three years younger than I, but was the most high-strung person I had ever known. He would lose his temper like lightning and fly into anyone, big or little, without warning. I had not been at my new home three hours when he leaped at me, and before I knew what was going on, mashed my nose as flat as a fried pie, and I began bleeding like a slashed hog. The sight of blood softened his fierce anger, and he ran to the house and brought a pan of water for me. We had many a fight during the succeeding years, in which no quarter was asked or given, but remembering that first encounter when I discovered what a hornet he was, I was able to protect my nose and to hold my own against his furious attacks. In the scores of fights we had during the next few years my advantage in height, weight, and years did no more than balance the scales against his quickness and fury.

I recall only one other fight when he caught me at a disadvantage. One day we were on the back of old Rufus with Walton riding behind. As we were crossing the big sandrock glade near our house, we began arguing, as usual, over some important issue, and I made a remark reflecting upon the sacredness of his honor. I had scarcely finished the sentence when lightning struck—he landed on my right ear with his fist. I reached back and punched him in the side. But as he was behind me he had every advantage. He pounded my ears, he mauled the back of my head, he pulled my hair, he beat my ribs. I saw myself headed for the ropes unless I changed tactics. So I jumped off the horse, intending to pick up a stick or rock and hove at him. But he hit the ground at the same instant I did, grabbed up the root of a black-jack sapling, and started to swing it round and round before flinging it. I began to dodge this way and that, and he kept swinging the root, which was as thick as his ankle. When he flung it, I threw up my hands to protect my head and caught the blow in the ribs on my left side. It was a knockdown. As I fell the thought shot through my mind to feign death. So I began to gasp and groan and roll my eyes.

When Walton saw my bloody shirt and my half-pretended agony, he bent over me and cried, "O, Johnny, Johnny, don't die, for God's sake don't die, and I'll never do it again; please, Johnny, don't die." He was in such a frenzy of fear that I eased up somewhat on my death struggles and began to come to, yet I knew the deception must be convincing lest he discover my pretense and come at me again with that blackjack root. Meanwhile he was making some solemn pledges about his future behavior. It was two full years before I told him I was shamming that day, and the effect was just what I expected: he charged at me with fists flying, and I responded in kind; however, no serious damage resulted.

When I was seventeen I taught a term of school near our home, and Walton was one of my pupils. I took advantage of my position to

even up old scores with him by giving him a licking in a perfectly legitimate way.

Put two growing boys together under the same roof anywhere, anytime, no matter how primitive the living conditions, give them a good deal of free rein, and if they are not crushed by cruel parents or cruel living conditions, they will find action, entertainment, and rivalry. So it was with Walton and me. Though we were "brothers," always together at work and play, always loyal to one another when troubles came, yet we were jealous, making sure that one never had an advantage over the other. For example, Walton liked turnips and I hated them, but I learned to tolerate them so as to keep him from getting my share. On the other hand, I liked beans and Walton did not, but rather than see me enjoy myself eating them, he cultivated a taste for them and was pleased to think that he was cutting into my supply.

We never had to look for entertainment. If we were not eating or working or pampering the animals or teasing them, we might be trying to follow a bee-line or playing games with the large green glade-lizards—very handsome creatures—that sunned themselves on sand-rocks all over the hills. Hunting bee-trees was an interesting pastime, and sometimes we were rewarded with rich finds. We always imagined that wild honey was finer-flavored than tame, just as we thought wild turkey meat was sweeter than domestic. To cut down a bee-tree when all the men and boys in the neighborhood are on hand is fine sport. Occasionally, however, our pastimes were more original and less innocent than following bee-lines or teasing lizards, and we sometimes paid a price for our rascality.

Though we managed to squirm out of nearly all the difficulties we got ourselves into, Uncle occasionally had to apply the corrective. When he found it necessary to whip us he cut two long dogwood switches—one for each of us—called us to him, took us by the left hand to make sure that we would stay with him during the operation, and applied the wood. When he raised the switch we always leaned backwards as far as possible without falling over, and at the same time bent our knees. This position had great merit, for it caused the slack of our pants to hang out quite a distance from our bodies so that the blow from the switch spent itself against the slack. The impact of the switch sounded like a man beating a carpet, but we scarcely felt it. We also learned right early to yell like Cherokees every time the switch fell. Our lusty outcries, coupled with the loud noise of the switch as it struck the slack of our pants, had the intended effect, for Uncle would think he was hurting us and would cut short the punishment or ease up on the energy he was putting into his work.

When the job was finished and he turned away, we would look at each other, wink the other eye, and laugh over the way we had fooled him. Once after we were leaving the scene of the ordeal, we became too eager to celebrate the deception. As Uncle walked away, we couldn't suppress our feelings and snickered so loud that he heard us. So he gave us an additional treatment that was much less amusing than the preceding one had been. Sometimes his distress over the sufferings shown by our whoops and yells was so evident that we actually felt sorry for him, and once or twice we were on the point of telling him he was not hurting us nearly as much as we let on; but at such times our self-control got the better of our sympathies and we decided it would be wrong to disillusion him.

One rainy morning Walton and I did not have to go to the fields to work, and as Uncle had gone to the mill, we had no chores to do. A tool shed stood back of the kitchen and we had access to all the tools. What boy doesn't love to handle augers, chisels, hammers, saws, gimlets, planes, squares, drawing-knives, screw-drivers, and the like?

We made full and indiscriminate use of the tools that morning, boring, sawing, hammering, one object being to make as big a racket as we could. We soon got around to all the ordinary tools and were about to run out of new noise-making apparatus, when we discovered an empty coal-oil barrel with the head knocked out. We turned it end for end, leaving the bottom end uppermost, and found that it made a tip-top sounding board. With two stout sticks we began hammering on the solid end of the barrel. The sound pleased us mightily, and we were happy to find that the harder we beat the sounding board the louder the noise. Soon we were making a continuous and hideous din, which got on my aunt's nerves, and she called out to us to "stop that racket." We usually obeyed her orders promptly, but this time we answered, "Wellum," and kept right on pounding the barrel end. In a moment or two we got a second command, which we answered with another "Wellum," and kept pounding away. For several days before this we had been absorbing some ideas from a hired hand, who had said that it was all right for women to rule inside the house, but they had no authority on the outside. We were easy converts to this way of thinking and were in favor of trying it out. Moreover, we could not see that beating a barrel head was hurting anything or anyone and so we beat it some more. But we overlooked the fact that Aunt was a person of very strong will power and that she had not accepted the hired man's point of view. About this time we heard her hasty foot-

steps coming out to the tool shed, and her sharp, impatient voice saying, "I'll stop it!" By this time she came in sight and we saw that she had in her hand a piece of plank about two feet long by six inches wide by one inch thick, and was taking aim to hurl it at us. We struck the barrel two last thumps and ran. Just as we got over the fence we looked back and she let drive at us with the board. Fortunately it missed us by about fifteen feet, as it was too heavy for her to handle with any sort of accuracy, supposing she had wanted to do so. But what she lacked in physical power she made up with her voice—she called us uncomplimentary names that were too accurate for our comfort.

Once we were safe from flying missiles it took us only a few minutes to conclude that we had been attacked, probably with intent to kill. Then we got to musing on the consequences if we had died from her onslaught. The thought of such a tragedy aroused our pity and our anger. Walton said, "Don't you wish to the Lord she had killed us both with that plank?" and I answered, "Think how the folks would look at us two little boys lying there in the same coffin and then they'd look at her and say to theirselves, 'You done it! you killed them little boys!' " The thought was more than we could bear, and Walton began to cry. I immediately joined him, and we both broke down and gave way to the most woeful sobs. Walton said, "They'd bury us out there in them lonesome woods," and we doubled our outcries. It was some time before we could calm our minds sufficiently to compare ideas on how near Aunt came to killing us both.

The arrival of my uncle from the mill put a sudden end to our weeping and wailing. He brought news about Will Rutledge's steamboat trip to Batesville, and we soon forgot our troubles. Luckily we escaped punishment for our misconduct, but on other occasions we were not so fortunate.

One day, in a moment of weakness, we discovered that cold biscuits and cream were not bad eating between meals, especially when indulged in on the sly. In the weeks following this discovery we very often slipped out into the kitchen, which was detached from the cabin, got some cold biscuits and table spoons, skimmed off some cream, and enjoyed a hurried feast. This pastime, which soon grew into a habit in spite of any efforts we may have made to shake it off, was attended with inconvenience as well as danger, and some of the zest was taken out of the feast because of the hurried manner in which we had to partake of it. Besides, it was inconvenient to wash the spoons until they were clean and free of all tell-tale signs of cream, and it was a bit dangerous to be prowling around in the kitchen after hours with spoons in our hands. So we transferred our activities to the spring house, three hundred yards away, where the fresh milk was kept in crocks, submerged up to the rim in cold spring water. Here we had more freedom of action, found a larger field for operations, and got a broader outlook on life, as the sequel shows.

The element of danger still was not entirely dissipated, for slipping spoons out of the kitchen and slipping them back again carried a certain degree of risk. Besides, it was a proceeding that lacked tone and dignity. Boys of our high caliber and broad views ought not to be hedged in by any such narrow restraints. We therefore conceived the idea of making for ourselves some unpatented cream-skimmers. We also fell upon the plan of slipping a biscuit or two into our pockets at meal-time so that raids on the kitchen could be entirely eliminated. We could hide our cream-skimmers and the stolen biscuits in or near the spring house and enjoy at leisure our between-meal feasts without any risk whatsoever; moreover, we would not have to wash our cream-skimmers after using them. The outlook was indeed rosy.

To make our cream-lifters we went to the tool-house. Walton made his out of a percussion cap box, drilling a hole near the top for a handle, which he made to fit tightly into it. It was a clever job. I was a bit more artistic in my skimmer. I got a piece of oak some fourteen inches long by three inches wide and two inches thick. At one end I chiseled out a cup two inches square and an inch and a half deep and shaved down the rest of the stick into a handle a foot long. I even worked an artistic curve into the handle. It was a rather clumsy-looking contraption, but in use it was very efficient. We looked upon our handiwork with feelings of pride and admiration. Not only did we admire the fruits of our labor, but we also admired ourselves for our genius and foresight in inventing them; moreover, we were under no obligations to anyone for borrowed spoons.

Every other day was our schedule for making raids on the spring house. Once inside, we would shut the door and proceed leisurely with the business in hand. At first we carried our skimmers out with us and hid them safely. But soon we grew careless and laid them on a high shelf, pushing them well back out of sight, a piece of carelessness which was a factor in our undoing. One day we discovered a tall jar of strained honey alongside the milk, put there to keep ants from getting into it, and we immediately expanded our field of operations. We were very grateful for this delicacy and added it to our bill of fare, for we found that biscuits and honey were larrupin' when washed

down with rich cream. Things were surely coming our way. Life, on the whole, was very pleasant. The universe was friendly. It was a good world to live in.

On one of our customary raids, we thought we heard someone coming and made a hasty exit, first scooping up two skimmers full of honey to take with us. The alarm was false, but outside where it was light, I happened to look at the honey in my skimmer as I was gulping down the last of it, and to my horror I discovered that it was full of small red ants—some dead, some dying, and others very much alive, trying to swim ashore. I supposed there were thousands of them inside us. The dead ones did not give us any concern, but we did not relish the thought of several hundred live ants gnawing and clawing inside our systems trying to find a way out. We tried to reconsider the situation by "heaving up Jonah," but the effort was fruitless. The ants made a good filler. Evidently we or someone else had done a bad job of covering the honey jar, leaving one end of the napkin which had covered it hanging off onto the floor, in that way making a perfect gang-plank for the ants from the floor to the top of the jar, and a million or so had committed suicide by diving off into the honey.

But our luck was too good to last. One black day we forgot to cover the milk crocks. When whoever handled the milk—I think it was my sister—found a crock uncovered, suspicions were aroused and an inquiry was set on foot. In fact, suspicions had been aroused before this because of the growing scarcity of cream, there not being enough on some days for the coffee, whereas on other days there was plenty. An investigation was quietly begun, and in nosing around in the spring house the folks found our cream-skimmers lying back on the high shelf.

We were haled into court and plied with leading questions. Our feelings were hurt that we were under suspicion. We did not know anything at all about the matter; in fact, we did not understand what they were talking about. If a crock of milk was uncovered it was no concern of ours. One thing we knew and that was we hadn't uncovered it. Our hands were clean, our consciences were clear, and we were ready to leave the witness stand and conclude the hearing. But we were detained and questioned more sharply. Hard-pressed, we promulgated what seemed to us a very plausible theory about the matter. In our opinion, a dog had left the milk uncovered. This suggestion looked good to us and seemed to clear up a rather foggy situation. But somehow the folks were not impressed with our theory. Skepticism bulged out on every side, and the difficulties protruded in front.

Uncle observed that if a dog had uncovered the crock, he was a most intelligent animal, for he had stolen the cream off two other crocks and had replaced the covers nicely. Moreover, he had latched the door after him when he went out!

The situation was getting complicated and began to look grave to us. Walton and I were thinking hard and fast. The dog theory had been left without a leg to stand on, and we were floundering around, trying to think up something, anything, to gain a little time. But at this juncture we were surprised, chagrinned, horrified, when Uncle produced two strange-looking utensils which had been found on a shelf in the spring house—left there, no doubt, by this same intelligent dog!

We were up a tree—Walton and I. Our lines of defense had been shattered. The evidence was all against us. Our cake was dough. There was but one thing to do, one last desperate expedient to invoke, and that was to turn State's evidence against each other. This we promptly did in the hope of securing something from the wreck, some little personal advantage. But it was a vain hope. "We were taken without the west gate and there punished according to the imprecations of our own mouths."

While loitering in the orchard one April day, Walton and I carved our initials on the soft, smooth bark of an apple tree and found the pastime very enjoyable, as our knives were sharp and the gray bark yielded easily, showing the white wood underneath. After completing our initials, we moved to other trees and cut our full names, improving in craftsmanship and style with each effort. Well pleased with our handiwork, we enlarged our field of activity by carving other words than our names, some of which were of questionable social standing. And finally, led on by the knavery that is typical of young boys, we proceeded with much pleasure to cut upon the trees of the orchard still other words, amusing words not heard in good company, terse and pithy monosyllables, verbs and nouns.

After gleefully adorning a number of trees with these bold words, we surveyed our work with pride and returned to the house more pleased than usual with ourselves and our participation in the things that make life worth living. During the next few days, we made several trips to the orchard to admire our work, and in going to and from the farm we went out of our way to catch a glimpse of it. We thought it was overwhelming, and beyond question the funniest thing any mortals ever did. Our cups were almost too full.

One Saturday several weeks later, a number of the Branscumb

boys spent the night with us. There were ten boys in the family, but only five came, as the others were too old to be interested in boys of our age. Our secret about the carving was too good to keep, so as a mark of special favor to our guests, we told them about our recent work and took them to the orchard to let them see with their own eyes the display of our skill and wit. We felt that the work was unique in both mechanical skill and literary excellence, and we encouraged the boys, as we walked along, to believe that by patient practice they might presently achieve equally satisfactory results on their own trees. But we told them frankly that there was no room for improvement on our literary performance, since we had used up all the funniest words we or anybody else knew.

On the following Sunday there was preaching at the church a quarter of a mile from our house, and as usual there were about twenty-five invited and uninvited guests at our house for dinner. In mid-afternoon the young people on the place grew restless, and four couples of them, including my sister, decided to take a stroll in the orchard to enjoy the shade of the trees and to look at the ripening fruit. Walton and I had no business traipsing along after these young men and women, as we were too young to be congenial; but boy-like we went along, lagging back well to the rear, yet keeping check on everything that happened.

As chance would have it, the young people walked directly to the apple tree with our names carved on it, where they quickly discovered our handiwork, and read our names. One or two of them made complimentary remarks about the carving, which pleased us mightily. But, unluckily, one of the company, Will Rutledge, who could neither read nor write, espied some carving on another tree close by and said, "See here, whose names is them?"

The young ladies and gentlemen hurried over to the other tree and thrust their faces up close to the words. There was a brief moment of cold silence. Then abruptly and without explanation, they hurried away. In confusion they turned to another tree, where equally scandalous carving met their eyes. Finally, in ill-disguised embarrassment and with flushed faces, they retreated from the orchard.

Walton and I had observed the whole proceeding and were in high glee; we could hardly restrain our laughter; in fact, we did snicker out loud several times. But I saw a cloud on my sister's face that boded no good for us. Our consciences began to trouble us, and our pride in the carving began a sharp decline.

There were no alarming repercussions at the supper table that evening and when nothing was said at breakfast table next morning, we felt that the situation had cleared up in our favor. When we went to dinner, everything was still going well, and we were feeling happy about the whole episode. But during the meal, Uncle, in his quiet, deliberate way, asked innocently enough, "Can you boys carve your names on an apple tree?"

The question elicited no information.

Then he asked me directly, looking me straight in the eyes, "John, can you carve your name on an apple tree?"

Reluctantly, I answered that I could.

Walton replied in like manner, weakly.

Uncle then asked, "Can you carve anything else besides your names?"

Again we guessed maybe we could.

By this time our appetites were gone, and we hurriedly closed operations, pushed our chairs back, and started to hurry out of the house. We were going to the orchard to obliterate certain carvings. But Uncle detained us. He said he would go with us out to the orchard, which he did, and took Aunt with him. Walking straight to the trees where the most shameful carving now stood out like banner headlines in a newspaper, he told us to spell out loud and pronounce the words. We spelled them but couldn't bring ourselves to say the words in the presence of Aunt. So we stuttered and stumbled and mispronounced them in voices that were weak and high.

Uncle asked us, "Did you boys do that?"

We hadn't. We were surprised that he would ask us such a question. Our feelings were hurt. We knew nothing for certain about the carving, but we believed we could name the guilty parties. In our opinion it was done by the Branscumb boys, who had spent the night with us just two weeks ago and had been in the orchard for an hour. But Uncle knocked the props out from under this suggestion by saying that the carving had been done several weeks ago, for the bark had commenced to roll over the exposed wood; whereas, if the Branscumb boys had done it there would be no such growth of bark. Thus was our solution demolished.

Then he wanted to know why we lagged back from the young folks when they were in the orchard and why we snickered out loud when they turned away from the trees with the carving on them. We couldn't explain. In fact, the whole situation was an enigma to us —we couldn't understand it. But my uncle could, and he proceeded to enlighten us with a long dogwood switch.

Thus did budding genius meet with cruel discouragement, right in its incipiency.

Though Walton and I were happy living at the Swans' we had our troubles. The regular Saturday night round of medicine, in sickness and health, was a torment that all children of that time and place had to endure, but it was not the worst. One of the most inhuman cruelties ever inflicted on a fourteen-year-old boy is this: after he has come home on a summer evening, dog-tired from plowing in the fields, hot and hungry as a mule, and has eaten his supper and slid down out of his chair onto the floor and dropped off instantly into slumber, profound and sweet—to have someone dig him in the ribs and say, "Get up, Johnny, and wash your feet and go to bed." I can prove that this is the essence of double-distilled cruelty by every country boy who has tried to sneak off to bed with dirty feet. We went barefoot from April to October, so our feet were nearly always dirty.

How often, O how often have I thought with indignation of this other cruelty: after Walton and I have eaten our noon dinners on hot summer days and have crawled under the bed where the flies won't bother us, so as to get a short nap before going back to the plow —suddenly to be jolted by a loud, sharp female voice saying, "You boys go down to the spring while you're restin' and fetch a bucket of water." Now in our case the spring was down a steep hill nearly a quarter of a mile away. As Walton and I sauntered forth, day after day, muttering complaints and maledictions on the head of any person who would call hauling water "restin'," we showed plainly the effects of injustice and injury, and we suspected that life was vain and illusory and hardly worth the living.

An even heavier burden for Walton and me, almost too heavy to bear, was the hired man who drifted into our backwoods community in 1878 and hired to work on Uncle's eighty-acre farm. We had just moved from the Bond place with its big orchard to the Franks place, a mile away, which had greater acreage and a larger cabin. Warren was about fifty years old, tall and dark, with gander eyes. He had a thin sharp nose and on the end of it there hung a globule of clear liquid from November to April, when it disappeared until cool weather came again. We promptly named him "Colonel" because of the prominent part he had taken in the Civil War, that is, as told by himself. Although he never said which side he led to victory in that great struggle, we suspected he had worn the blue, if indeed he had fought at all, which we seriously doubted.

Walton and I developed a robust dislike for Mr. Warren on several counts. First of all, he was much too industrious. He loved to work and did his best to keep us at work for much longer hours than we thought reasonable. He got us up and out into the field too early in the morning and kept us there too late in the afternoon. Also he ate too much to suit us, although we had all we wanted to eat and didn't have to provide any of his food. His diet consisted mainly of food we didn't care much for: cornbread, bacon, cabbage and turnips. But to see a man we disliked enjoy himself so heartily three times a day was almost too much to bear. At every meal he drank six cups of coffee, black and strong. After his third cup he would say to Aunt, "Jist a drap more, jist a drap," which meant another cupful, his fourth, and likewise with his fifth and sixth. Now we always had plenty of coffee, bought green in one-hundred-and-thirty-five-pound sacks, parched in skillets, and ground by Aunt. Walton and I didn't drink it, but Warren's heavy consumption of it kept our minds constantly on edge. Aunt made about a gallon for every meal, and at supper a pint or a quart would be left in the pot. Early every morning, winter and summer, Warren would go straight to the coffee pot, even before he dressed, and turn it up and drain it to the grounds, no matter how cold or strong the coffee might be. When we had biscuits—Walton and I loved them—Warren never stopped at less than twelve, even when he was not feeling very well. When his health improved he ate a good many—and in doing so strained our endurance to the breaking-point.

Another fault we found in Warren was his way of telling a bigger tale than the one he had just listened to. If someone told a good story, Warren would fidget in impatience to get started with his own yarn. We were sure he stretched his tales or probably invented them. A good many dealt with his heroic War experiences. He had a long muzzle-loading rifle that he said he had carried throughout the War and had used to kill many an enemy soldier. To illustrate what a center-shooting gun his rifle was when he handled it, he told us this story. With some assistance he had just routed the enemy from a stronghold, and as he was approaching it to take it over, he saw a big fellow about three hundred yards away jump up from cover and start running. Warren took aim "right whar his galluses crossed" and dropped his man. Since his rifle would carry only two hundred yards, Walton and I put a heavy discount on this story, as we did on his other military exploits.

Warren also gave himself a high rating as a hunter, but aside from killing a wild turkey now and then he never showed any evidence of his prowess. He made frequent mention of the big game he had killed along the Gasconade River in Missouri and of his accuracy at spearing fish in that river. Walton and I talked these claims over and allowed, privately of course, that the Gasconade River was a muddy stream, too muddy for fish to be seen; that there were no fish in the Gasconade; and that if there was such a river it was in Illinois or Dakota, not Missouri.

One afternoon in late summer he took Uncle's double-barreled shot-gun and went out into the corn-field. In about a half-hour we heard both barrels of the gun go off almost simultaneously. Presently he walked into the yard with five turkeys about three-fourths grown hanging over his shoulder as he held them by their heads. The flock had been taken by surprise and were running down a corn row, single file. Warren had dropped to his knees and fired both barrels at their heads. Our entire family gathered about him and the pile of turkeys, expressing surprise and admiration for his unusual feat. Walton and I joined in the general acclaim; but immediately we noted in him a pose of indifference to our compliments that chilled our enthusiasm. He made a few disparaging remarks about killing five turkeys at one time, as if it were too trivial and commonplace to call for more than momentary notice by a real hunter. He seemed bored by our excitement and in the midst of our compliments asked Uncle when he thought the ground ought to be broken for sowing the winter wheat. Walton and I conferred about Warren's conduct and quickly agreed that he was a hypocrite and a scoundrel, that he had never before performed any feat of hunting comparable to this one, and that the compliments of the family were sweet music in his ears.

Our bitterest grudge against Warren was the way he had of tattling on us to Uncle whenever we were negligent in our work. He would not tell on us directly but would take a devious course in giving us away that aroused our indignation and wrath. One day the three of us were working in the new corn patch—he was plowing and Walton and I were digging out the sprouts that had sprung from old roots —when Old Bragg came chasing a rabbit across the field and into a hollow tree in the woods beyond. Walton and I had our enthusiasm for work under good control, so we left the field to twist the rabbit out of the tree with long dogwood switches. It took us an hour or so to get the rabbit, and we went back to the field, proudly showing the live animal to Warren. He made no comment and took no interest in our exploit, all of which caused us to think that he was going to tell on us for losing so much time from our work. At the dinner table that noon he asked innocently, "Did you boys get that rabbit you went after, down in the woods?" Of course he knew we got it, for we had shown it to him and explained how we twisted it out of the tree. If he wanted to avoid our dislike he might as well not have resorted to this shabby trick of asking an apparently innocent question. Uncle took note of the query and made an investigation which ended when he gave us a mild lecture with a dogwood switch.

Warren's outrageous treatment of us rankled within us as long as he was with us, and even after we grew up and went separate ways we would talk about Warren whenever we met and express our hearty contempt over the way he had acted about the turkeys and the rabbit.

Chapter IV
Fashions for Boys in the Leatherwoods

The visits of strangers and people of prominence in our community such as the doctor or the proprietor of the store in the village of Calico Rock, several miles distant, were events of much importance in the lives of country boys back in the Leatherwoods during the 1870s. Walton and I were always glad to have strangers drop in on us, provided they wore clothes that we considered good and didn't eat too much. When someone we knew and admired came to our home, it was like a school holiday. As unexpected as a bolt from the blue was the coming, one Saturday, of Dr. J. A. Kerr, the schoolmaster of Spring Creek. He appreciated the good spelling records Ellen and I had made in his academy, and to show his appreciation he came to see us in our new home at the Swans'.

Professor Kerr rode a fine fox-trotting horse. He was as usual well dressed in "store-bought" clothes—not home-made, like ours. His light brown hat was of the stove-pipe variety very proper in those days and about as tall as the plug hats of a much later time. I admired Dr. Kerr greatly. I had told Walton everything I knew about him and probably a good deal that I didn't know, so that we were in a fine state of mind to appreciate and enjoy his visit. We would not have been nearly as pleased if President Hayes or Queen Victoria had come to see us. Not the preacher nor even the doctor was so important in our eyes as Dr. Kerr. We were doubly pleased when he agreed to stay until Monday morning.

Walton and I sat as close to him as we could and followed him around constantly in order to look at him, study him, admire him, and hear everything he said. We lingered over every syllable he spoke, and when he completed a remark we looked at one another in happy approval, delighted at the wisdom imparted. Ellen and I were elated when he mentioned our good spelling records, and we hoped that the other members of the family were impressed. It would be quite impossible for any other person to understand what a treat his visit was to us. Walton and I raced to have the honor of feeding his horse, showed him our treasury of old magazines, and waited on him as though he were an imperial guest. And we dreaded for Monday morning to come—but come it did, and the family followed him out to the gate to say goodbye.

Walton and I had a way of boasting about being the last to see anyone or anything of interest or to enjoy any rare experience. If we got to go to the river to see a steamboat land, each of us would boast that he was the last to step off the boat or that he saw her last, just as she went around the bend. So while the other members of the family were bidding adieu to Professor Kerr, Walton and I sauntered off down the road so as to catch the last possible glimpse of him. There was no advance notion or agreement between us about this move. Willie had slipped away quietly, unseen by anyone except me; I knew very well what he had in mind, and I followed. Professor Kerr quickly overtook us, bade us a cheery goodbye, and hurrying on at a lively foxtrot was soon out of sight. Then things began to pick up for Walton and me. Competition and prevarication ran high. We took out after the Professor, first at a lively walk, next at a fast sprint, and finally at a dead run.

In the lead, Walton suddenly said, "I seed him last just as he went over the hump in the road."

I knew he hadn't, but the contest was on and I must not be beaten in a matter so important. There was no time to waste and nothing to be gained by arguing the point; so I ran past Walton a few steps and yelled, "There, I just seed him as he passed by the big sassafras tree."

In turn Walton gained a lead on me and hollered, "I seed him go 'round the bend on the other side of the tree."

As soon as I recovered my breath, I sprinted ahead of Walton and leaped high with the claim that "I got a good look at his back as he went into the woods across the sandrock glade."

We were too diplomatic to question each other's veracity, although each of us knew full well that the other was doing some tall lying. Quibbling and contradiction would only confuse the situation and jeopardize the important purpose each of us was trying to gain.

Walton again dashed past me and caught a glimpse of Dr. Kerr's tall hat through an opening in the woods. "And you couldn't see him because you was behind me, and he's plumb out of sight now."

But I hopped up onto a three-foot sandrock, and though I could not see any farther down the trail than I could from level ground, I

craned my neck and yelled, "I seed him plain as he went out of sight the other side of the rise. You can't see him no more on account of the hill."

But Walton could, it seems, and so could I. Each of us caught several more glimpses of him. So we kept up this running and lying until we were out of breath, by which time our visitor was probably four miles away and we a mile and a half from home.

Walton and I were not particular about the kind of everyday clothes we wore. In the summer we wore two garments: a shirt and a pair of breeches—that was all. In winter we wore neither vests nor overcoats. Belts were unknown, but we wore galluses, frequently one gallus hitched to our breeches with a small wooden peg or a horse-shoe nail. And, of course, we had warm woolen coats. Like all clothes worn by country boys of the period, ours were home-spun, made by the women of the household. In our case, my aunt and the two girls, Ellen and Annie, carded the wool or cotton, spun the yarn on an old-fashioned spinning wheel, and wove the cloth on the old-fashioned handloom. Aunt had two pairs of cards; Uncle paid $7.50 for one pair and $50.00 for the other—all in Confederate money. Aunt always cut out our clothes by guess, and her guesses were often not even close. One time our pants would be so tight that we could hardly get a leg into them and so short that they struck us half-way between the knee and ankle. Our coats would be equally tight and the sleeves several inches too short. We looked like rubes—which we were. The next time Aunt would remember how badly she had guessed the last time and would make amends by cutting out coats and pants "full." This was especially true with the pants. They would drag the ground, and each pant leg would be large enough to hold both legs; the coats would lap across half a foot in front, and the sleeves would be three inches too long. All we had to do, Aunt said, was to roll them up. When we complained about our ill-fitting clothes, we were cheerfully reminded that we would "grow to them," all of which was more or less consoling to Walton and me.

> We praise her biscuits and her pies,
> Her doughnuts and her cake;
> But where's the man who sighs for pants
> Like Mother used to make?

Mrs. Swan was very resourceful in dyeing the cloth she wove to be made into clothes—woolen for the boys and cotton for the girls. She used red oak bark or black warnut (walnut) hulls to dye the cloth black; hickory bark to get a yellow; lichens or moss that grew on the

flat sandrock of the glades near our home to furnish a fine brown color; and madder to get red. She added a bit of alum to make the yellow of the hickory bark "set." Red clay was sometimes used to turn white cloth or thread to an orange color. All this coloring matter provided a variety of checks and stripes for the cotton dresses, jackets, and capes worn by the girls and for the pants and coats of woolen cloth made for the boys.

Attired in our homespuns year after year, Walton and I were well satisfied with our every-day apparel. But we always took note of the way other folks dressed on Sundays, and we wanted to dress like them if we admired them and unlike them if we disliked them. Once we had a hired man we despised because he waked us up too early every morning; he buckled his suspenders so high that his pants came up close under his arms. To show our disapproval of him, we let our suspenders out until our pants hung very low, threatening to fall off our hips. But if the men we admired wore something out of the ordinary we took careful note and wanted to dress like them—as well as talk and act like them.

Among the lingering memories of Dr. Kerr's visit was that of a long-tailed duster he wore that came below his knees. These long-tailed coats were quite the popular garment for men of importance to wear during hot weather, just as the Prince Albert was popular in the 1880s. The fact that Dr. Kerr wore a duster on this visit was all the evidence Walton and I needed to give importance and class to this garment and to insure the high social standing of those who wore it. Before many days passed we began to pine for long-tailed dusters. It did not occur to us that boys were not supposed to wear this kind of coat; even if other boys never wore them, what of it? Did not Dr. Kerr wear them, and was not he the model and the standard for everything?

Walton and I wanted coats just like his as much as we ever wanted anything in our lives, and nothing less than long-tailed dusters would satisfy us. It seemed to us that if we could have coats of the same pattern and color and length as Dr. Kerr's, we would look exactly like him and rise to the heights of prestige in the neighborhood. Certainly we would attract a lot of attention and be the envy of every boy in the City Rock community. We therefore set upon my uncle until life for him must have been a burden. Our entreaties prevailed. The next time he went to Pineville, ten miles away and across the river, he bought the material, an unusual favor since our clothes had always been homespun. Then we had trouble getting Aunt to make them, for no one in north Arkansas or perhaps any-

55

where else had ever seen small boys wearing tails to their coats as long as we wanted—or for that matter, tails of any kind. We were concerned that someone in our neighborhood would have dusters a foot or two longer than ours, so we inveigled Aunt into dropping them to our ankles. As was her practice she cut the coats by guess, and her guesses were as random as ever. I was much larger than Walton, so she made mine large enough to wrap around me twice, and Walton's so tight it wouldn't meet in front. But whatever they lacked in fit and comfort and beauty they made up in length. Today, after sixty years, as I think back on our being given these ridiculous coats, together with not a few other things we set our hearts upon, things we did not need, I am amazed at the indulgence and the patience of my uncle and aunt in gratifying us boys.

We heard there was to be preaching at Cold Water the second Sunday in August, and we immediately asked and got permission to go—with this understanding: we could take only one horse, old Rufus, and we would both have to ride him. At once the question arose of who would ride in front and who behind. Being more than three years older than Walton and considerably taller, I felt that to ride behind a smaller boy, with my head towering up four inches above his, would be a shock to my dignity amounting to a major calamity. My grand debut into the world of manly fashion would be spoiled: I might as well be dead. I argued to Walton in the strongest language I could command that custom directed the older and taller to ride in front, that it would be contrary to all time-honored precedent for me to ride up behind him. He was so impressed by my argument that he said I would have to whip him if I rode in front. This was a call to arms, and hostilities broke out at once. While we were fighting, landing on jaw, chin, ears, and chest, Uncle suddenly was standing over us. Now nothing could cool our tempers and cement our friendship more quickly than the appearance of Uncle, no matter how bitter the conflict. So we explained to him that we did not mean anything personal at all by our exercises when he came up, that we held no ill will against one another, but were simply having a little disagreement over who should ride up behind when we went to Cold Water. The argument was resumed, but with less heat.

Walton admitted that I was older and larger, but insisted that we should go as equals, that one should ride in front going and the other returning. That was a fair proposal, but it did not suit me at all. I said that I would never go to Cold Water Church riding behind Walton. He countered by saying that I could take my choice of riding or walking. The prospect of walking four miles to Cold Water with Walton mounted in his finery on a good horse did not look at all right to me, and I suggested that we split both trips in half and take turns riding in front: to show how fair I could be I would let him ride afore the first two miles going, and I would ride in front the first two miles returning. This proposal sounded fair to him and he readily agreed, not realizing that I would ride into and out of Cold Water in the position of honor, and that we would probably not meet a soul on the two miles of the road nearest our home, when he would be in front.

This important issue settled, we could hardly wait for the second Sunday in August to come, when we would go to church and show off our handsome coats. We hoped that the service would be well attended and that we would attract the attention of every human eye in the Leatherwoods. Our hopes were abundantly realized—much too abundantly. At the ages of twelve and nine, with dusters that almost dragged the ground, Walton and I must have been a sight for the gods.

We rode up to the church in happy expectation, but the people who were loafing outside did not give us the warm, admiring looks that we had expected; they stared at us as if we were prize calves at a county fair. After we dismounted, they wagged their heads at us and pointed their fingers at us. When we saw their glances of disapproval and amusement, we realized with sinking hearts that our dusters were having the opposite effect from that intended and so confidently expected. As we walked toward the church, men and boys gathered in small groups to make remarks in low tones and jerk their thumbs over their shoulders at us. At length a young man and two boys openly snickered at us. This was the last straw; and Walton, always quick-tempered and high-strung, gathered up some rocks and began pelting our tormentors, while I backed up to the trunk of a tree and sat down against it, a seat I occupied during the remainder of the morning. No such miserable day was ever spent by two would-be style-setters. We would have gone home at once but for the thought that we would have had to give an explanation to the folks—and this we could not do. When at length we did return and were questioned by Aunt and Uncle we had little to say; but we were happy to get out of our dusters and into our jeans. Before we wore our dusters again we had a yard cut off the tails.

In April, 1878, Uncle bought Walton and me straw hats, for which he paid twenty-five cents apiece. They were plaited, checkerboard style, with alternate stripes of purple and natural straw, and were exactly alike except that mine was one size larger than

Walton's. We were not taken to the store and fitted, for the store was over the river and ten miles away, but the sizes were guessed at. In those days and in that center of human affairs, as I have said, shoes and hats were bought—all other apparel was home-made.

I took a fancy to Walton's hat for the sole reason that it was smaller than mine. I always wanted a hat to perch high up on my head; Walton, on the other hand, wanted his hats to come down low and rest on his ears. I did not let Walton know I admired his hat or had designs on it because that would have precluded all possibility of getting a swap out of him. Our methods of dealing with each other were devious, and complicated, and involved. And so I began a systematic and persistent campaign of criticism and fault-finding with his hat, pointing out from time to time the glaring defects in it, at the same time calling his attention to the total absence of any such defects in mine. This approach fell on deaf ears at first, for he held up stoutly for the virtues of his hat and was likewise blind to those points of superiority that I claimed for mine. But fortune favored me when one day Walton got caught in a shower and the brim of his hat persisted in turning up fore and aft. He had been wearing his hat turned down in front and up behind. As usual I wore mine turned up all around. I was not slow in calling his attention to the way his hat brim now turned up and I harped on it continually, remembering the old proverb:

> Water, dripping day by day
> Will wear the hardest rock away;

and I made good use of it. So Walton began to show signs of weakening, and in the course of ten days or two weeks, he was ripe for a trade, although he kept his feelings concealed from me. But one day after I had delivered myself of an unusually strong and forceful harangue on the topic, Walton asked me, in the most careless and indifferent sort of way, how I would like to swap hats with him, just as though a brand new idea had flashed into his mind, having no connection with the arguments I had been propounding so assiduously for the past six weeks. With a forced indifference that would have done credit to an expert poker player, I replied that the superior virtues of my hat were so obvious to any unbiased mind that I could not think of swapping—unless very substantial concessions, in the way of "boot," were made to me. I followed this up with the further remark that I guessed there was no chance for us to make a trade, since I had a hat that pleased me in every respect and there was no good reason why I should trade it off, especially for an inferior one, so full of faults and shortcomings. Walton scoffed at the idea of giving "boot," and we dropped the matter for the time being.

Willie and I had always listened with the keenest interest to the business talk, the trade talk of our elders. Occasionally a neighbor, J. D. Dozier, visited us and he and Uncle would talk money talk—the low price of cotton, the going price of cattle, the high prices of the merchandise at the newly-opened store at Calico Rock. Live-stock buyers from Missouri bargained with Uncle over the cattle he had for sale, and now and then a neighbor bought a cow or two, sometimes on credit. Walton and I always stood around while negotiations were going on, and not a word escaped us. After the deals were closed, we talked them over wisely and knowingly. We had loitered in the stores of Will Rutledge and Joshua Bond and had watched every sale made and had heard talk of terms, collections, and hard cash. We had listened to creditors demand payment of debts and debtors ask for more time. Rutledge had been more than willing to tell us how he bargained for his stock of goods with merchants at Batesville, where according to him, he had made some very shrewd deals. We had heard Jim Herd say that a neighbor of his had made $800 "clear money" on his cotton, and that Bill Bradford had gone south on a buying trip with $1200 in money on him. Expressions like "clear money" and "money on him" sounded good to us and we held on to them. From such conversations as these Walton and I learned the vocabulary of high finance, which we put to good use in our hat trade.

Two or three days after our first discussion Walton renewed the suggestion of a trade, as I confidently hoped and believed he would. This time I told him frankly that I could not afford to trade with him on anything like equal terms in view of the vast gulf that separated the two hats in style, quality, and general appearance. With equal frankness Walton then asked how much "boot" I would expect in case he should become interested in a trade. I replied that while I cared nothing at all about swapping off my hat, yet to accommodate him and to show the proper spirit I would swap, but could never, under any circumstances, bring myself to take a cent less than ten cents clear money to boot.

The proposition of ten cents boot was preposterous to Walton. He would go bare-headed all summer before he would pay any such exorbitant sum; he wouldn't even consider it and we might as well drop the matter. It was evident we could not get together that day, and so we dropped negotiations for the present. Within two or three days the subject, which was gnawing at our vitals every hour we were awake, came up again. Walton said that while he had not budged an inch from paying any such amount as ten cents and never would budge an inch, yet he might become interested in paying a smaller and more reasonable sum. I instantly and eagerly asked him how much smaller. He replied that in order to show his good faith and his perfect fairness, he would be willing to pay a difference of five cents, but said that I must act quickly, as he could not hold such a liberal proposition open indefinitely. I made him a counter-proposition to the effect that I would "split the difference and take seven and a half cents to boot." This offer went on the rocks when he reminded me that he had no half-cent pieces. In truth he had as many half-cent pieces as he had five-cent pieces, for he had neither.

After further negotiations, propositions, and counter-propositions, we traded—on Walton's terms—that is, he agreed to pay me five cents difference. I knew very well he did not have five cents, and had no way of getting it, so I demanded that a date be set, at which time full payment should be made. He agreed to pay me not later than Christmas, which would give him five months to raise the money. I thought the time too long and told him that everybody settled up in the fall—say by November 15—and that I would be willing for the account to run until that date, provided he would make every effort to pay me sooner than that. He agreed to pay me as soon as he could get the money, whereupon we joyfully exchanged hats. My newly-gained possession rested even more highly on my head than I dared hope, and his all but swallowed him.

We were both happy over the trade, and the debt of five cents became the occasion for more big talk between us, as well as a subject for frequent wrangling. It was not more than three weeks until I began to dun Walton for the five cents, although I knew very well he did not have a red penny. At first, I dunned him once a week, on Saturdays; then twice a week; then once a day or even more often. The usual set-to would be about like this:

"Now, see here; I want that money you owe me. I've waited on you long enough. I need my money."

"Well, John, you know I ain't got no money on me now, and besides I said I'd pay you Christmas. You know I'm good for it. I never owed no debt I didn't pay, and you know I'm goin' to pay you."

I would then remind him that circumstances alter cases and that owing to changed conditions I was now in straightened circumstances, and nothing but ready cash would relieve me; moreover, he had promised to pay me off before Christmas in case he made a raise.

To this Walton would reply, "You know I've been turnin' every wheel I could to raise some money. I've got some deals on right now to raise it, but it takes time. By this time next year I'll be in fine shape."

"How'll you be in fine shape?"

"I'll be standin' behind the counter."

"Yes, you'll be pullin' a plow-line across old Beck—that's how you'll be standin' behind the counter."

Presently we would wear the subject out and drop it when our stock of big talk was exhausted. But the next day it would break out afresh: "You know the money you owe me,"—I never mentioned the amount; it was always "the money" as though it were ten thousand dollars—"well, I want you to pay it off. I can't wait no longer. I've got to have it. I'll give you just five more days. If you don't settle up by that time, something is going to happen."

Walton would counter with: "John, you know I've not got that much money right now. What's the use for you to dun me? I aim to pay the last cent just as soon as I make a raise."

"When will that be?"

"Well, a man never can tell. I may be broke today and next week have plenty of money. It comes and goes."

Sometimes the argument took a turn like this: "Willie, how about that money you owe me? You owed it now nearly four months and the debt is just as big now as it was at the start. Besides, I haven't got a scrap of paper to show how much you owe me. What if I'd lay down and die—what shape would I be in then?"

"You'd be dead—but I'll pay that debt. All my life I've paid my debts. There's no man livin' can ever say I beat him out of a dollar. That's not the way I make my money—by beating people. Right now I'm poor but I'm honest, and some of these days, before very long, I'll have more money than I know what to do with. Then you'll be following me around tryin' to borry money from me."

And so it went from day to day, and from week to week, and from month to month. My recollection is that he failed to raise the money by Christmas, but in the following spring he sold a rubber ball to me for five cents and thus liquidated the debt, along with a grudge which had caused a lot of wrangling between us and one or two fights.

After Walton and I were grown and married and lived in different towns, we and our families, Ellen and her family, and other relatives occasionally got together—about twenty in all—and at these reunions our children always called on Willie and me to tell about our boyhood pranks. First one of us and then the other would reminisce

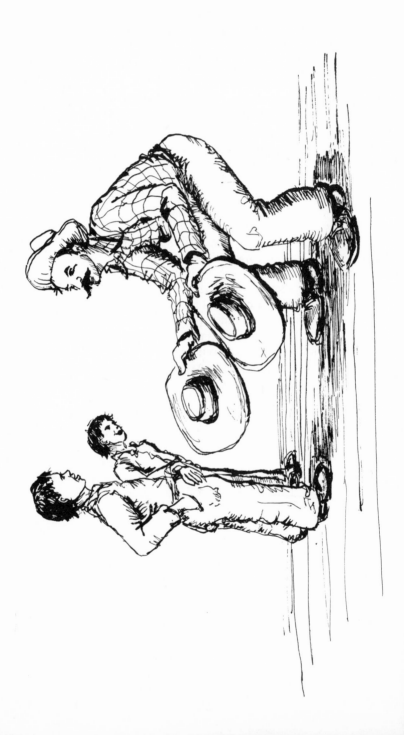

until the whole party laughed to exhaustion. I recall more than once seeing tears of laughter roll down the cheeks of some of the young men and women. The hat trade was one of the favorite stories, and we needed no urging to tell it as a side-light on high financing in the Leatherwood Mountains in the 1870s. If Willie were here he could help me liven up many a page of these reminiscences and remind me of incidents that have slipped my memory, but unfortunately he died a few years ago in California.

William Rutledge, a farmer who lived two miles from us, had a handful of goods to sell, mostly to renters. From a trip down the River to Batesville he brought back two of the broadest-brimmed black wool hats I ever saw—never even saw a sombrero with a brim quite so broad. Walton and I admired those hats and wanted them; they caught our fancy instantly. On the way home from the store we laid our plans to get Uncle to buy them for us, in case he should put up any resistance—a most likely prospect. In the first place, we needed the hats. Those we had were worn and dilapidated, not the kind of hats that boys of our parts ought to wear. In the second place, the big hats would shelter us from the weather—rain and snow in the winter and rain and sun in the summer. The brims were so wide that they made perfect umbrellas for any season of the year. In the third place, they were only two dollars each and being made of wool would last for several years. In the fourth place, if we should lose them the finder would readily identify them, as there were no other such hats in the Leatherwoods.

Yielding to pressure, Uncle gave us four dollars and we hurried back to Rutledge's lest he sell the hats to someone else. He still had them. We put them on and started for home in a run, eager to have the family see us in these noble top-pieces. Willie turned his brim down in front and up behind; he had to turn his head upward at an angle of thirty degrees before he could see out. I wore mine with the brim up all around. The folks at home were waiting for us. The girls, Ellen and Annie, saw us first and instantly broke into laughter. The sight of us rather small boys under those enormous hats—the brims must have been fourteen inches wide—was too much for them. Walton and I were irked. We told them hotly they didn't know anything about how men's hats ought to look. Aunt and Uncle came in while we were arguing, and although they tried to keep from laughing, they could not hide their amusement, and Walton and I began to feel that the four of them were misguided and backward in their sense of style and that the other folks in the neighborhood would admire and envy us.

The following Saturday we asked if we could go to the Post Office for the mail, which came once a week. Usually only one person went, but we both wanted to go so that neither would have any advantage in showing off his hat. At the Post Office three women had come for mail, and we overheard one of them say, "Lord, I wish you'd look at them hats them boys has got on; that little one's hat'll break his neck." She referred to Walton, who was short and skinny. The second woman asked, "What on earth is that on his head, nohow?"

During the next two or three weeks we heard other unkind comments about our hats. But we persisted in wearing them, hoping for an upturn in community opinion. At church men and boys gathered around us; they all seemed to be in unusually good humor, eyes twinkling, smiles on their faces. We didn't have anything to say. They did. One asked us if our necks were sore. Another said there was one advantage in having such big hats—that if we wanted to get across the River and there was no boat handy we could ferry across in them. Remarks of the same tenor, which we thought exhibited a very low order of wit, uncomplimentary remarks, unfeeling remarks, cutting remarks, words not fitly spoken, continued to fall upon our ears until life lost its savor.

In due time we put our heads together and gave out the information in the neighborhood that if anyone wanted to buy two broad-brimmed black woolen hats, he could learn something to his advantage by seeing either of us at the Swan residence. Within a week after we reached this decision, two young men bought them—at a discount. It was a relief to escape from an unhappy situation with so little permanent damage to any of our family.

In the spring of 1879 a peddler, the first one I ever saw or heard of, came our way with a large bundle on his back. He opened up his pack and spread out his goods on the front porch. The novelty of the visit appealed to the whole family, and we gathered around him to look at his wares. We did not really need any of them, but Uncle bought some things for the girls, trifles that struck their fancy. Usually country boys did not come in for much consideration in matters of this kind—they never needed anything. But the shrewd peddler was not long in stirring us boys until we spoke out. He took a look at us and said that we were just the right age to have some nice Sunday breeches. Now Walton and I had not been interested in Sunday breeches—we had no idea we needed Sunday breeches. Up to now we had been entirely contented with our jeans woven by Aunt and the girls. But immediately we realized that the peddler had spoken the truth: we direly needed some new pants and by all means ought to have them. In fact, we saw that we couldn't get along much longer without them.

Luckily the peddler had just the thing for us. He unrolled a fabric and began to expound on its unique merits in a most convincing way. It was a pale blue-grayish piece of goods. It would not tear, would not fade, would not shrink. It would wear like iron, although it had a very soft finish. He gave it the picturesque and attractive name of English moleskin and said it was beyond question the most appropriate goods for boys' pants ever imported from England or anywhere else. Walton and I wanted pants made from that cloth. Our mouths began to water and our eyes to brighten. There was one minor point, however, that needed explanation: the material smelled like a fertilizer factory or a sack of Peruvian guano. We raised a question about the rank odor. With cheerful assurance the peddler said that that was the material's strong point! perhaps its strongest point! It was the natural odor of the mole and was all-sufficient proof, if any were needed, of the genuineness of the material and at the same time a guarantee of its wearing qualities, its durability. He said furthermore that every boy in the country would want a pair just like ours as soon as we wore them in public. He had only a yard more than it would take to make the two pairs of pants, and he would sell us the extra yard at half price if we would buy the rest of the goods at ninety cents a yard. He told us that the odor, which he did not find at all offensive but pungent and stimulating, would disappear the first time the pants were washed.

Uncle bought the material, and in due time it was made into two pairs of pants that fit us very well except for being too full in the rear and several inches too short. However, the fit of the breeches was of little concern to us, since they were made of genuine English mole-skin. We were especially pleased with the stripes which ran down the legs because we recalled that when Dr. Kerr had visited us his pants had the same kind of stripes.

The folks at home, Ellen and Annie in particular, did not share our enthusiasm for the breeches. When we wore them about the house they did not care for our company. They spoke their minds freely about the odor, and were so unkind as to hold their noses as we passed by them. But we disregarded all such childish teasing and waited impatiently for "meetin' day," when there would be preaching at the church four miles away. By and by the third Sunday arrived and we proudly donned our moleskin pants and were among the first to arrive at the church. We stood off by ourselves outside the building to give all the churchgoers the opportunity to see and admire our pants, and we entered the church late so as to call attention to ourselves. When we went in, we sat down beside some men, who almost immediately became restless. They looked at us inquisitively and one of them sniffed several times as though trying to locate the source of a strange odor. Then one of them whispered something, and they all got up and moved several seats forward, out of range. Presently three women came in and sat beside us. At once they began to look at one another in an uneasy sort of way. One of them examined her shoes to see if perchance she had stepped in something or other. They looked at us very searchingly and then moved to the far end of the bench. A man on the row in front of us turned around and gave us an ugly stare over his shoulder. Across the aisle a boy made a face at us that said as much as words could have done. During the rest of the service we ignored those about us and looked steadfastly at the preacher.

Back home we had our pants soaked for hours, washed with the strongest lye soap, and sunned all day, and we fancied that the smell had lessened. But our hopes were vain. Wherever we went the moleskin odor went ahead of us—in fact it was in circulation when we arrived—and our presence was not appreciated. Luckily, in about a month we heard of two boys living not far away who had only rags to wear for breeches. Our hearts were touched, and in an outburst of charity we sent our moleskin pants to these unfortunates. The other members of our household gave their hearty approval to this evidence of our brotherly kindness.

Chapter V
Dreams and Characters

Dreams were never taken lightly by the pioneers in the Ozarks—often very seriously as warnings or revelations of things to come. Out of a very great many dream-stories that I heard during my early years, some of them many times, I will relate two. The first one I have called "A Thousand Dollar Breakfast."

One night my grandmother Wolf had a dream that upset her badly. She dreamed that she was standing out in the yard and saw a large black snake coming towards her, its head erect and its tongue darting menacingly. When within a few feet of her it stopped, raised its head, turned quickly, and went away in a different direction. In a few moments it reappeared coming from still another direction, again stopped when it got within ten feet of her, and again retreated in a different direction. A third time it appeared, stopped, raised its head, and disappeared.

The next morning at the breakfast table she asked her husband, my grandfather John Wolf, if there was any unclaimed land in his two hundred acres of river bottoms. At first he said no, there was none. "Are you sure?" she insisted. After a brief silence he said, "Yes, there is a forty west of the well that is unclaimed, but no one knows about it, and if they did, none of my neighbors would run under me and homestead it. How come you ask?"

Then she told him about her dream and said that the snake looked like one of their neighbors. She was sure, she said, that her dream was a warning that this neighbor was about to homestead the forty that was unclaimed, and she asked Grandfather to get on his horse and go to the Land Office at Batesville, where he could enter the land on the books. He did not set much store by her dream and interpretation, but she was so insistent that he finally consented to get up early the next day and make the trip to Batesville, sixty-five miles away.

Soon after daybreak on the following morning he saddled his horse and was on his way, and when darkness overtook him he was within nine miles of Batesville. He spent the night at a farmhouse, got up early the following morning and told the farmer he was in a hurry and would not stay for breakfast. When he reached Batesville the Land Office had not opened, so he took his stand at the door and waited till the clerk came. Then he went in and stated his business. The clerk looked up the land numbers, made out the papers, and receipted my grandfather for the fees. As grandfather went out the door, one of his nearest neighbors went in. Grandfather later learned that this neighbor had tried to claim the identical "forty" which none of the people in the area were supposed to know about.

The neighbor had spent the night at a farmhouse about a mile from where my grandfather had stopped. But he had stayed for breakfast and by so doing had lost his chance to get the forty acres. His breakfast cost him $1,000, the value of the land he lost.

My second story took place thirty or forty years before I was born, when lawless frontiersmen hunted and traded up and down the White River.

In late summer when Jim Grant pulled up to his home on the bank of the Ohio in Kentucky after spending most of the spring and summer on the White, he found his wife in trouble. She said she had been molested by the Trimble brothers, Bill and Watt. James Grant took his wife to the home of his parents and went back to his canoe. Down the Ohio he went, down the Mississippi to the mouth of the White, up the White to a trading post near North Fork, and there he found Bill Trimble. Bill was suspicious and wary, but Grant greeted him in a casual way as though he knew nothing and suspected nothing. "Whur you been at?" asked Trimble.

"New Orleans," said Grant.

"What doin'?"

"Sellin' hides."

"You ain't been to Kaintuck?"

"Nah," said Grant.

"How's the folks in Kaintuck?" asked Trimble.

"Ain't heerd. But I'll be goin' back in a week or two."

Within a few hours the two men had planned a hunting trip down the river. They went in Grant's canoe with Trimble's tied behind it. Jim brought along a keg of whiskey, and Trimble drank, but Grant did not, though he pretended to do so. They stopped at Hawthorns' on Moccasin Creek for midday dinner, later the I. H. Talley place.

While they were there, Hawthorn's mother, a very old woman, broke out in a warning to Trimble. "They's a rock in a corner of our field as big as a house," said the old woman. "I dreamed I saw an owl settin' on that rock, and hit dropped down dead, and I went to it, and hit was you, Bill Trimble."

Half-drunk, Trimble laughed at her story. The two men left Hawthorns' in the afternoon and at dusk stopped at a house three miles above the mouth of Calico Creek, where the Carter women lived. After dark Grant pretended to be pretty drunk. He swore he was going on down the River that night, picked up his gun, which he called Jack o' Diamonds, and walked out of the house. Trimble followed him out and persuaded him to come back, but when Grant re-entered the room, he did not bring Jack o' Diamonds with him.

Up to this time Trimble had carried his rifle, named Sweet Lips, in his hands or rested it across his knees. Now walking unsteadily, he leaned his rifle against the fireplace and sat down in a chair. Grant picked up Sweet Lips and once more walked out the door. When Trimble followed him outside, Grant shot him through the heart with his own gun, Sweet Lips. He then returned to the house and told the women, "Sweet Lips has spoken a big word, but Jack o' Diamonds will soon speak a bigger one." He tried to calm the Carter women and told them that the Trimble men had abused his wife in Kentucky. With no more delay he left the house, turned Trimble over to make sure he was dead, and walked down toward the River.

Grant was not heard of again until he reached Watt Trimble's place at the head of Trimble's Island in the lower White. He landed, went up to the house, and found Watt dying of tuberculosis and unable to walk. He told Watt, "I killed your brother Bill up at the Carter women's place and came here to kill you, but your Maker is killin' you fast enough." So Jack o' Diamonds never got to speak the big word that Grant had promised. He left Watt Trimble dying, got in his canoe, and was never seen on the White River again.

Meanwhile some of the settlers living on the upper White took Bill Trimble's body and buried it at the foot of the rock big as a house where old lady Hawthorn had dreamed that the owl swept down dead onto the ground. I revisited this spot recently and found the big rock still there, but nothing else marks the place where Bill Trimble's dust lies.

Sparsely settled though the Leatherwoods were, they had their share of "characters." For example, there was Johnny Wooten, who was thought to be a kind of wizard or trafficker in magic. Wonderful tales were told of his deeds in wizardry, and Aunt was afraid of him. He brought his dead work animals back to life and encountered strange creatures in the woods. And there was "Patting Billy" Hixson, distantly related to the other Hixsons, who incessantly drummed with his hands or feet. Uncle Jackie Trimble, a unique character from a neighboring county, was widely known for his political speeches. During a campaign for the legislature he laid claim to superiority over his opponents by priority of citizenship, declaring on the stump that in the early days he had heard the "angry roar of the lion, the fierce scream of the panther, and the heavy tread of the elephant" resounding in the hills long before his opponents had set foot in them.

Another political worthy was the Honorable Byrd Smith, who lived fifteen miles away across the River. Since he campaigned for Congress nearly every two years, unsuccessfully, we occasionally saw him. He was fairly well-informed on public affairs, had a strong voice, could speak unendingly on any subject, and had a sure remedy for every ill of society. But government finance was his main interest and the main topic of his conversation and his speeches. He was a Greenbacker, and in his campaigns for Congress Greenbackism was his platform. His opponents for office traveled by horse over our two-hundred-mile-wide district, but he always campaigned on foot. He met his opponents promptly at every appointment and never failed to make his two-hour speech. About once a year he would appear unannounced at our cabin, and though we did not charge him for bed and meals, he paid us in work if there was need for his services. An excellent clocksmith, he inspected our time pieces without our asking, and if either one of our two clocks was out of order he would take it apart and hunt till he found the trouble. Always he left our clocks keeping good time. His regular defeats at the polls disappointed but never discouraged him, and after two years he was ready again to preach his saving gospel of the Greenback to an unbelieving district.

Mr. Turnbull drifted into our neighborhood from the mountains one summer day when we were in the midst of a "protracted meeting" being conducted by the Reverend J. J. Vest. He claimed membership in some branch of the Baptist denomination, but became deeply interested in Brother Vest's preaching and asked him to preach a doctrinal sermon. The request was granted and at the conclusion of the sermon he asked to join our Missionary Baptist Church and be baptized in the White River, two miles away. The usual, more convenient baptismal spots did not suit him. He said he would appear for the ordinance the following Sunday riding on an ass. In an effort to comply with his wishes, a site on the River at the mouth of Jackson's Creek was chosen, and a search was made in the community for an ass. But no one owned such an animal. The outlook for the baptismal service became discouraging as the date drew near and no ass could be found. Nevertheless a large crowd gathered on the bank of the White River on Sunday afternoon and a bit of excitement was in the air.

About half-past three in the afternoon word passed quickly through the crowd that Mr. Turnbull was coming. And sure enough, in a moment he hove into the view of everyone, mounted on the very animal he had wanted, his feet almost dragging the ground. Somewhere back in the hills he had found one, an undersized one, and as he was lanky, the two of them made a good show. By the vigorous use of a hickory switch he got the animal into a trot as he struck the edge of the crowd and scattered the people in making a path to the edge of the water.

Brother Vest lost no time in getting him into the River. Turnbull wanted to speak to the crowd, but the preacher led him quickly into deep water and submerged him; then hurried him out of the River and back to the ass. The newly baptized brother mounted the ass and was soon out of sight headed back into the hills. Brother Vest's rather highhanded tack doubtless deprived our community of at least a mild sensation on that Sunday afternoon.

"Aunt Polly" Hixson, a plain-spoken, energetic German housewife who cooked unusual German dishes, was one of the foremost of the Leatherwoods people. For her, life was never slow, couldn't be slow; she must be doing all her waking hours, else she would die of boredom. Neither man nor beast nor devil could intimidate her, though the Devil made at least one attempt to do so. One night as she was walking along a lonely path to the home of a neighbor, she found her way blocked by a shape that looked somewhat like a big dog, so long that it extended across the path and into the woods on either side. It was black and heavy and shiny. Its hideous mouth was open, showing huge teeth as red as fire. Its eyes gleamed like balls of fire. Though she was afraid of nothing, she chose not to invite trouble by running into the monster and instead walked around it. Yet no sooner was she back in the path than looking ahead she saw the same shape blocking her way, as ugly as before. Again she left the path and walked around it. Back in the path she quickened her pace, hoping the beast would not overtake her, but suddenly it was there once more blocking her way. By now her patience was exhausted and her ire was rising. She resolved to have it out with the creature without further delay. So she rushed at it with all her strength and kicked at it where she supposed its heart should be. But she struck nothing and fell headlong in the path. Scrambling to her feet, she looked about her, but the monster had vanished and appeared no more. When she arrived at her neighbor's house and told her story, the men and women of the household lighted torches and went to where Aunt Polly had fallen, but they saw nothing and found no tracks except her own. She maintained it was the Devil that she had encountered.

The most unusual character of my acquaintance was Joshua Bond, who came into the Leatherwoods about 1855 and homesteaded forty acres of land in 1860. He was a well-educated man, a university graduate, who was said to have sustained a broken vertebra during an athletic contest, an injury that disfigured his back and embittered him. As a result he left his family and friends and made his home in the Leatherwoods for the rest of his life, with the exception of five years in the Northwest.

He chose to homestead one of the roughest, most forbidding forties he could find. Here he built himself a modest home of hewn yellow-pine logs. Directly in front of his cabin rose a hill several hundred feet high, and on the northern slope of this hill he planted a large orchard consisting of over a hundred trees—apple, peach, pear, plum, apricot, quince, and cherry; also three acres of strawberries, blackberries, raspberries, and grapes. As this orchard was on the north side of the hill, it never budded out early in the spring, and consequently he never had a crop failure. I recall, after sixty years, several varieties of his apple trees: Winesap, Twenty Ounce, Bellflower, Smokehouse, Limbertwig, Sheepnose, Red June, Early Harvest, Cider, Crab, and Lady. The Lady was exceptionally fine, a small, flat, thin-skinned, highly-colored apple that snapped like chocolate bonbons when bitten into and had a delightful spicy flavor that I have never tasted in any other apple. I also remember three varieties of peach: Stump the World, White Heath, and Indian. The last was bright red throughout and its juice just as red.

As Mr. Bond had no market for any of this fruit, hundreds of bushels of fine peaches, apples, and other fruit ripened and fell to the ground and decayed under the trees. He refused to give any of it away to anyone—visitor or neighbor. Consequently his acquaintances said that he was the most miserly and stingy man they had ever known.

Once in conversation with my mother he expressed the wish that when he came to die he could convert all his property into a pile of gunpowder and touch a lighted match to it as he drew his last breath. Mother asked him if he would not prefer to give his property to widows and orphans. He replied that widows and orphans had not helped him to acquire the property.

In 1872 he sold his house and forty acres to my uncle, Mr. Swan, and opened a store at Calico Rock. While so engaged, he boarded with us (my mother, Ellen, and me), and though I was only eight years old, he impressed me with his knowledge of a universe that I knew nothing about. He taught me the twelve constellations of the zodiac, and to this day I remember them; he talked of the incredible size of the sun and stars and their equally incredible distances from the earth. I became so interested that I was well prepared for the great comet of 1881, which I still consider the most impressive sight my eyes have ever beheld, and for the transit of Venus, which I watched, spellbound, through smoked glass on December 6, 1882. When I grew to manhood the stars became a hobby I have followed through the years with never failing interest.

Mr. Bond was the most rapid talker I have ever listened to. While speaking he took offense if interrupted, and in case his listeners showed any sign of indifference, he stopped and spoke his displeasure. Once while he was discoursing in his usual manner on some period of history, my mother cautioned a child about making too much noise. Instantly he stopped and said sharply, "I presume my conversation is not very interesting." At another time when he was speaking at his headlong rate, one of his audience let his eyes wander away from him and out the open door. Mr. Bond fairly snapped, "Listen to me while I philosophize!"

He did not continue long in business at Calico Rock, but decided to sell all his property and to go to the Northwest. Among the things offered for sale was a handsome clock about two feet high with a glass case which exposed the works to view. When no one was willing to give his price for the clock, he carried it to the River where a ferryboat was tied to the bank, walked to the far end of the boat, and heaved his beautiful clock into the River.

In a few years he returned from the Northwest and put in a small stock of goods at the Table Rock Post Office, two miles from his former home, and here he lived alone. Every six months he shipped to Senter and Company, an old commission house in St. Louis, all the country produce he had accumulated, such as ginseng and golden seal,* hides, furs, beeswax, and tallow, and once a year he went to St. Louis to settle with the company and bring back with him a stock of merchandise to last the following year. He was scrupulously honest. Mr. William Senter once told me that he would not hesitate to advance Mr. Bond as much as $2,000. But Bond never went into debt.

He was considered an expert in locating underground water courses, but I do not recall that he used the forked stick of the water witch. At the base of the hill where he set out his orchard there was a sluggish seep-water spring within a hundred yards of his house. He dug back into the hill, following up the small stream; then he got three or four spring lizards and put them in the stream. These wriggled their way back into the hill, following the veins of the spring, and in a few days the flow became bolder until a good free-flowing spring was streaming from the hill and has continued ever since. In later years he sold his place and built a cabin a half-mile away, but there was no water on the place. He chose a low spot a hundred yards from his cabin and dug down about five feet where he struck water. Again he got some spring lizards and put them into the pool. In a short time it was overflowing and became an unfailing spring.

When old age was drawing near, Mr. Bond made a profession of faith to the Reverend J. J. Vest, of Calico Rock, the pastor of our backwoods church, and asked to be immersed, on the condition that there should be no witnesses except Mr. Swan. The next day Mr. Swan hitched up his two-horse wagon and took Mr. Bond and the preacher to a mill-pond one mile above the mouth of Jackson's Creek, and here Joshua Bond was immersed, presumably with only one witness. It is not easy, however, to escape the eyes of a growing boy when his curiosity has been aroused. Walton took note of the mysterious preparations being made and followed the wagon with its three occupants to the millpond, and hidden behind a clump of bushes watched the baptism of this eccentric man.

Mr. Bond died as he had lived, alone, leaving his modest home and some money and other property, which were claimed a few years later by relatives from Missouri. He had no close friends and no enemies and was held in high respect by all who knew him.

*Both are medicinal herbs.

Chapter VI
Wild Life and Weather Lore

I arrived in the Ozarks too late to do much big game hunting. The buffalo had disappeared and the black bear was no longer plentiful. In the early days, the heavy growth of cane that covered the river and creek bottoms made good cover for wild life, in particular for the bears; and the limestone caves in the hills were perfect dens for the big blacks. Arkansas has been called "The Big Bear State" because of the celebrated hunts here early in the nineteenth century and more directly because of the publicity given the Arkansas bear by such nationally known writers as Fent Noland and Thomas B. Thorpe. A village on the White River with the unusual name of Oil Trough is a lasting monument to the big bear hunts of the early days. Beginning about 1800 the area in and around the present site of Oil Trough was a favorite hunting ground for the French frontiersmen who came up the White once a year in pirogues and wide canoes and camped in the bottoms. On one of the first of these hunts it is said that they remained for several weeks and killed more than a hundred bears. The kill was so great that they soon filled all their available containers with oil*

---

*Bear's oil was used by the French in New Orleans for cooking and salads in place of olive oil. In the northern territories it took the place of butter. Timothy Flint (*History and Geography of the Mississippi Valley*, 1832) thought it "mild and agreeable to the taste when not rancid." According to Flint, it was floated downriver to New Orleans by filling one pirogue with oil and lashing it to another one with the boatmen. The Reverend James B. Finley (*Pioneer Life in the West*, Cincinnati, 1853) describes bear hunts in Kentucky at the turn of the nineteenth century. He writes: "After dissection, the alimentary canal has been found to contain from one to two gallons of oil. This oil is pure and unmixed." Dr. Simeon David Bateman, physician and

and had to improvise rude vessels to store the surplus while they waited for boats to transport it to New Orleans. So they cut down the largest trees near the camp and hollowed out ten- to thirty-foot lengths of the trunks for use as storage tanks, some of them holding two hundred and fifty gallons of the oil. During the following years, overflows of the White River carried the tree-trunks here and there in the bottoms, where they hung in cane brakes and thickets. Forty years later two or three of them were still near the old campsite. Early in the century they had become a landmark and had given a name to the locality. When a village eventually grew up there, a name was waiting for it—Oil Trough. It is still on the map, eighteen miles below Batesville on the White River.

Though the early hunters killed most of the bears in the river bottoms, and the pioneers and later settlers cleared up and farmed the rich low lands along the river where the black bears had been most numerous, many of the big animals still lived in the creek bottoms and wild country back in the hills. In mid-century a few professional bear-hunters were still active, of whom my grandfather Adams* was one. He sold or traded both skins and oil to keel-boatmen operating on the river as far up as North Fork. His hunting grounds were the Buffalo, the Leatherwood, and the Sylamore Mountains, and on his hunts he always took his dogs, including several trained by himself. When he went into a cave for a bear he always left his dogs outside at the mouth. In case he wounded a bear inside the cave it would immediately break for the mouth to make its escape. Owing to the difficulty of holding up his torch to take good aim with his rifle, he occasionally failed to make a fatal shot, and the bear would come charging out past him. But it could not escape the sentinels at the mouth of the cave, for they would surround it and dart in, seize its hind legs, and as quickly dart out of reach of the dangerous paws, in this way keeping the bear from escaping until the hunter came out and shot it.

On a never-to-be-forgotten hunt my grandfather followed a bear to the mouth of a cave, left his dogs at the entrance, lighted his torch, and went in. He came presently to a narrow opening, where he could

---

planter at Oil Trough in the mid-nineteenth century, recalls (in S. W. Stockard's *The History of Lawrence, Jackson, Independence and Stone Counties,* Little Rock, 1904) that the oil troughs were floated in rafts to New Orleans. He goes on to say: "Bear's grease was as good as butter. We used bear's oil in place of lard and ate it like molasses."

*John Quincy Wolf's maternal grandfather, Thornton Stroddard Adams, died near Calico Rock in 1845 at the age of 37.

scarcely squeeze through into the wide passage beyond. About a hundred yards past the narrow passage he discovered the bear lying down thirty or forty feet away, against a ledge of rock. He took aim and fired, but he did not hit a vital spot and the bear quickly charged down the passage. My grandfather tried to outrun the bear and get past the narrows before the wounded animal reached them. But the bear overtook him right at the spot, slapped the torch out of his hand, and both man and beast started through at the same time. Of course the bear won the battle and crowded past him. In doing so it squeezed the breath out of my grandfather so that he collapsed and lost consciousness lying on the floor of the cave. It was about two hours before he came to and recovered enough strength to make his way forward. He could see the dim light of the entrance, and he felt his way toward it. When he finally reached the mouth of the cave he found that his dogs had halted the bear and were charging its hind feet and legs every time it attempted to run. They had worried it until it was well-nigh exhausted. Grandfather quickly reloaded the gun and killed the animal. Thereafter when he went hunting he always took someone with him to carry the torch.

In 1873 Tom Hamilton, a neighbor living two miles from us, built a pen about three hundred yards from his cabin to fatten up his hogs for his year's supply of meat. Late in December he missed one of the hogs, which weighed about two hundred pounds, and he suspected that the theft was perpetrated by some neighbors who lived three miles away. The following week another hog disappeared, and since the rails of the pen all remained in place he felt certain that the thief was a two-legged animal and that unless he acted promptly he would have no spare-ribs, backbones, and sausage that winter, and no lard, bacon, and hams the following summer. He decided to use his large-bore muzzle-loading rifle in arranging for his thieving neighbor to shoot himself the next time he got hungry for pork. Tom drove a forked post into the ground about three feet outside the pen, and in the fork he secured the gunstock. He laid the barrel of the gun on a fence-rail and tied it down tightly. Then he strung a cord across the pen high enough so that the hogs could not touch it as they walked about in the pen and tied one end of the cord to a fence rail and the other to the trigger of the gun, which was cocked and ready to fire. Any man walking about the pen would be certain to strike the cord, discharge the gun, and put a bullet in his thighs or legs.

Being a bit nervous over the possibilities and afraid to go alone to the hog pen in case the rifle fired, Hamilton got Dick Partee, another neighbor of ours, to spend the night with him. About nine o'clock that night the ancient rifle boomed out a loud report that echoed and re-echoed through the surrounding hills and valleys. Having no lamp, Tom lighted a long pine torch, and the two men walked cautiously to the pen where they found the hogs in commotion. Peering over the top of the pen they saw a large black bear sprawled on the ground, dead. He had committed suicide by shooting himself through both kidneys; his weight—four hundred pounds. Mr. Hamilton did not miss any more hogs.

My own first acquaintance with a bear came about unexpectedly. Wes Bunch, a stringy six-footer who grew up in the Leatherwoods, was tramping through the forest one October afternoon in search of bee-trees. While following a "bee-line," he suddenly spied two very small cub bears. They were too young to get away, so he quickly grabbed them up. But they were not too small to set up vociferous cries of distress. While Wes was deciding what his next move would be if Mama Bear appeared, he heard her come crashing through the woods, rattling leaves and breaking dry sticks under her feet. Wes at once concluded his deliberations, shoved the bears inside his shirt, sprinted for a slender hickory sapling some yards away, and ran up it with the agility of a squirrel. By the time Mrs. Bear got to the tree Wes was twenty feet up, adjusting himself to a limb that grew out at a right angle to the tree, as most upland hickory limbs do. Mrs. Bear could not climb the sapling—it was too small. Had the trunk been large enough for her to reach her paws around and get a firm hold, she could have given Wes no end of trouble. As it was, he had trouble enough, for the bear sat down at the foot of the tree and stared up at him steadfastly for three mortal hours, waiting for her prisoner to come down. The usual order was reversed in this case, for instead of the man treeing the bear, the bear had treed the man.

It was growing late, and Wes was weary and anxious—wondering who was going to win this waiting game and how he was going to spend the night, with a hickory limb for a bed and two squirming, clawing young bears for bedfellows. Finally when the sun was only half an hour high the bear walked off slowly and hesitatingly into the woods. As soon as she was out of sight Wes very cautiously climbed down, and, taking a cub in each hand, he "lit a shuck" for home, not stopping to investigate how far he was in the lead of the bear, but ran until he was sure he was out of danger. He did not see the mother bear again.

A few days later he gave one of the cubs to Uncle. In the Swan home the little bear was fed, petted, and pampered until he thought the place belonged to him. He was short and fat and chubby, nearly as wide as long, and he wore a thick coat of curly hair. Neighbors came to see him nearly every day, and he became a very popular bear. A friendly little fellow he was, always ready to play and to eat. He hankered after sweets in particular, but would not turn down milk and butter and gravy and meat—or bugs. One of his favorite pastimes was nosing around in visitors' pockets, hunting for something to eat. This little trick of his amused the children no end.

Christmas Eve night he was sleeping quietly on the wide hearth in front of the wood fire while the family group were sitting around in a semi-circle, admiring him, discussing his looks, his pranks, and his character in general, when he suddenly became uneasy and restless. He began to whimper and whine as if he were having bad dreams, which he undoubtedly was. Then waking up with a start, he began to scamper around the hearth, dodging aimlessly here and there, to our great amusement, almost running into the fire, until he came to himself. We thought he must have been dreaming of that day when Wes Bunch snatched him away from his mother.

One Sunday afternoon a month or two after this, the family went some miles away to church, to be gone until late in the day. The cub, now grown quite a bit larger, was shut up in the house to keep him from running away when he was alone, and to keep passing dogs from attacking him. During the long hours he became restless and made an investigation of the house, which turned out to be very interesting to him. He tore up the place generally, upsetting everything that was movable. In a corner of the room he found a crock of honey with a cloth tied over the top. He ripped the cloth away and ate all the honey, smearing it all over his paws, face, mouth, ears, and body. Then, apparently looking for something to wipe off the honey, he spied the end of a pillow-slip hanging over the edge of a bed, tore open the pillow, and strewed feathers all over the floor, the bed, the chairs, and himself.

When the family returned home, we were almost speechless when we opened the door and found the house in chaos—clothes scattered, bottles and chairs upturned, feathers all over, and honey on everything. Then the oddest-looking little animal we had ever seen ran to greet us. With his hair matted with honey and white feathers, he looked like a four-legged frizzly chicken. We all laughed off and on for half an hour at his comical appearance before we undertook the job of cleaning up the room—and him.

But this humorous escapade had a rather unhappy consequence. The Swans realized that the cub was growing up and that they could not shut him up in the house alone. Nor was it convenient or wise to take him along when the family went to church, lest he prove to be a greater attraction than the preacher. And it was only a matter of time until he might become dangerous. So Mr. Swan sold him to a man living twenty miles away, and we saw him no more.

In addition to bear, many kinds of wild life abounded in the Leatherwoods and often invaded our property. It was not unusual to see fifteen or more deer in a drove or twenty-five wild turkeys in a flock. Very often we heard wolves howling in the woods at night, but we rarely caught sight of them. Contrary to popular belief, timber wolves are not dangerous to man and they do not run in packs—at least not those in the Leatherwoods. If they ever harmed anyone, I did not hear about it, nor did I ever hear anyone say he saw a pack of wolves—unless a pair with two or three cubs or pups can be called a pack. But a family of four or five prowling the woods at night and making the darkness hideous with their barking sound like thirty and give one the shivers if one is not used to them.

Everyone in the Leatherwoods had encounters at one time or another with members of the cat family. Once when Uncle was out in the barn shucking corn he heard his three dogs break out in the wildest sort of barking on the hillside above the barn. They were giving some kind of animal a lively chase and soon treed it. Uncle thought they were after a squirrel which had ventured to visit his corn crib, and he went to the house for his rifle and shot pouch, expecting to have squirrel for supper. When he reached the tree where the dogs were barking, he could not see any kind of animal. The tree, a large white oak, was on a steep hillside, and Uncle climbed up the hill above the oak so as to get a better view of the upper branches. Unexpectedly he found himself looking into the eyes of a large panther lying on a limb not more than twenty feet away. He raised his rifle and ordinarily would have hit the panther in the eye, but in his excitement he made a poor shot—the bullet struck the panther in the end of the nose —whereupon it screamed, jumped off the limb, and ran up another tree, with the dogs in loud pursuit. Uncle reloaded his gun and made another poor shot, again hitting the animal in the face. Once more the panther screamed and ran up a third tree. This time Uncle took careful aim and shot the big cat in the heart. He said that he never saw a bigger panther—it measured nine feet from tip to tip.

Late one afternoon a year or two later Uncle heard a flock of wild turkeys in a small field of ungathered corn near the house. He got his rifle and slipped cautiously toward the turkeys, but they heard him and ran about three hundred yards up a dry branch. In response to a call from Uncle they halted and huddled together. From behind a clump of bushes he shot at this cluster of heads, not singling out any particular bird. When he fired, all the turkeys flew away except one, which flounced about on the ground. Uncle walked slowly up to the dying bird, not thinking to reload his gun, when suddenly a big catamount leaped with a cry upon the turkey, put one foot on the bird and spread its mouth in a snarl, showing its sharp teeth. This unexpected turn so upset Uncle that when he loaded his rifle and fired he missed the catamount entirely, although it was only fifteen yards away. But it was frightened by the report of the gun and slunk quickly about thirty yards away, sat down, and once more fixed its gaze upon Uncle. He hurriedly reloaded and laying his rifle against the side of a tree and shooting straight and true, deprived the beast of its turkey and its life.

A neighbor of ours, Smith Talley, had been hearing turkeys in his corn patch for several mornings just at dawn. At about the spot where he thought they had been feeding he found turkey tracks and set a trap, which he felt certain would catch one, and baited the trap with shelled corn. The following morning when he again heard the turkeys in his field, he got his gun and slipped along a thickly grown-up fence row that screened him from them. Crawling within fifteen yards of the birds he lay on his stomach, carefully selected the biggest gobbler among them, and fired his gun at its head. Quickly he climbed the fence and found the dead turkey bleeding at the head —with its feet held securely in his trap.

Farmyards in the backwoods were and still are subject to raids by various kinds of thieves, including 'possums, foxes, minks, rats, and chicken hawks, night-flying hawks, owls, and snakes—and all of these like the taste of chicken. The foxes, 'possums, minks, rats, owls, and certain species of hawks make their raids by night. The chicken hawks and snakes are daylight thieves. With all of them we had our troubles, mostly too commonplace to relate. One incident, however, was out of the ordinary.

Our chickens roosted on the lower branches of shade trees, choosing the horizontal limbs so as to sit comfortably. The belief was current in the hills that owls and night-hunting hawks do not swoop down upon a chicken and carry it off as do the chicken hawks —possibly because a chicken on a roost clings to the limb and squawks when attacked. They have a better plan of operation. The bird lights on the limb between the chicken and the trunk of the tree and begins to crowd the chicken out toward the end of the limb. The plans works well, for the chicken does not relish the idea of sitting close to a total stranger who isn't congenial. So the chicken yields and the visitor keeps crowding until they reach the end of the limb, where the chicken has no more room, and the limb becomes so small that it cannot hold up the two birds. The outcome is that the chicken slides off and instantly the predator swoops down, seizes the chicken in its talons, and flies away. Whether this is a mistaken backwoods notion or accurate natural history I do not know, but as it is well suited to the story of a hawk that made an error of judgment in our yard, I will assume that it is true.

We had some chickens that roosted in a post-oak tree just back of the kitchen. We also had some guineas that roosted with the chickens, and among them was a proud, high-stepping guinea rooster that claimed a conspicuous place on the roost. One night a hawk invited himself to this tree and happened to perch alongside this guinea rooster, doubtless pleased with the happy prospects. Immediately the hawk began the crowding operation, and presently the guinea fell, the hawk clutched him in fond embrace and flew away in triumph, with the guinea loudly telling his troubles to the world. Early the following morning we missed our guinea and supposed that he was a casualty. But about nine o'clock a strange mangled fowl limped into the yard, looking not at all like the nattily-dressed guinea that had been the dandy of the place. This bird had lost about half of his feathers, he had some ugly gashes on his sides and back, and his head was battered. But he was home.

Walton and I made a search for the battleground of guinea and hawk and found it on the hillside about a quarter of a mile from the house. And what a battle they had fought! Hawk and guinea feathers littered an area of some thirty feet square. The trail of feathers showed that the guinea broke away—probably when the hawk became battle-weary—and ran for his life to a projecting rock ledge where he hid and waited for day, then made his way home. I wonder if the hawk ever figured what went wrong with his modus operandi.

In the early days almost every farmer in the Ozarks owned a few guineas that dressed up his yard with their sporty attire and added life with their loud voices. At egg-laying time the guinea hen behaves far more subtly than the chicken. When the chicken hen is making plans to lay her egg, she doesn't care who knows, or how much her preparations are watched by the curious. She walks deliberately to her nest, and in the process of laying an egg she looks as grave as a justice of the Supreme Court. But when the egg is laid her behavior is suddenly changed. She startles you by jumping from the nest with a loud whoop and flies down to the floor or ground with a squawk that can be heard far beyond the farm, and for the next half hour celebrates her accomplishment with such a cackling and yelling as would almost waken her deceased forebears. Her boisterous conduct is so out of harmony with her quiet, serene life at other times that you are inclined to doubt her integrity.

Now when the guinea is ready to lay her egg she doesn't walk to her nest in full view of spectators. Not she. She lies to you about her intentions. She mingles casually with her friends, and when she sees that they have become interested in food or the weather and are paying her no attention she slips off quietly in exactly the opposite direction from her nest and after getting out of sight she makes a wide semi-circle so as to get around to the opposite side of the yard from where she started. Then she disappears into a blackberry thicket, where she lays her egg. Never even a whisper escapes her. After completing operations, she goes back quietly by the same route she came, walks up to the barnyard family unnoticed, and starts the conversation right where she left off, trying to give the impression that she has been there all the while.

If you ever find a guinea's nest, you will have to keep your eye on her for an hour before she starts to the thicket, and then as you follow her you will have to conceal yourself behind trees, stumps, and bushes, never letting Mrs. Guinea get out of your sight and never letting her get sight of you. After she disappears into the blackberry thicket you must wait until she emerges on the other side, and then, maybe, you can find her nest with about two dozen eggs in it.

Guineas are hardy, sleek, beautiful birds that decorate any farm yard. The chief objection to them is that they will fly up on the fence and yell for two hours at the tops of their loud, raucous voices about absolutely nothing.

Now, hunting quail is quite a different matter from hunting guinea hens' nests. One Christmas season before I went to live with the Swans our family was visiting the John Hursts, relatives of ours who lived year Yellville, Arkansas. Mr. Hurst loved to hunt. I recall that one night he went hunting for coons and brought in eight before ten o'clock. One of his neighbors had found a grove of trees where hundreds of quail roosted and had planned a big quail hunt for the holidays. The way to catch quail on the roost, so he said, was to put brimstone torches on the ends of cane poles and hold the torches under the roosting birds. The quail would soon be overcome with the fumes and fall into sacks which members of the hunting party were to hold open under the perches. The hunt was organized, and I was included in it. Everything went well. The quail were found, the torches held beneath them, and the sacks opened. But the birds were either ignorant or unmannerly, for they refused to fall down into the sacks. Instead of sitting quietly and inhaling the sulphur fumes until stupefied, they took one sniff and then flew away to other trees. We came home with empty sacks. (I am aware that quail habitually roost on the ground.)

I don't think I have ever been asked about the favorite topics of backwoods conversation, but if I should be I would answer, "The same things everybody everywhere talks about, in particular, the weather." Really, the weather came in for more than the usual amount of talk. We had no reports to tell us what tomorrow was going to be like, and had to do our own forecasting. This was important to us, as the weather was a very big part of our lives and our fortunes. Everyone had his own weather signs, and some of the short-range forecasts and forecasters were pretty reliable, but the long-range prophesies were nothing more than interesting talk.

Every fall great flocks of wild geese flew south. The weather prophets, taking note of this practice which the geese have been following for centuries, would declare that we were going to have one of the hardest winters in the last hundred years because the geese were flying in November and very high. (They always fly very high and in November.) Another prophet would inform us that we were going to have one of the worst droughts the country ever saw because last night he noticed a circle around the moon containing five stars. Another would announce that we were in for a bad winter because the squirrels were putting on an unusually heavy coat—always a sign of coming blizzards.

Every spring some of our prophets foretold the approach of a disastrous drought because the new moon was standing on its point, thereby showing that the water had already run out of it and left it dry as powder. An opposing school of forecasters maintained that we could expect a rainy summer and fall—so wet in fact that the crops would mildew—because the new moon was standing on its point, showing that it was going to pour out great floods of water. I heard of a backwoods prophet who said he had been watching the weather for forty years, and had noticed that if it didn't rain on the Fourth of July it always rained afterwards.

The weather also gave the old-timers of our neighborhood opportunities to exaggerate disasters of past years. If we had high water, one or more of them would always put in the withering remark: "Shucks, you ain't seed no high water. Jist orter seed the flood of '44. This here rise is jist a spring freshet beside it." And if we mentioned the big freeze of 1879, an old-timer would come up with something like: "Think that was cold weather, do ye? Well, if you'd a seed the winter of 1866 when all the chickens' legs froze off and the milk froze in the cows, and when you throwed a gourd full of water up in the air and hit come down like hail-stones, you'd a knowed what cold weather is."

Chapter VII
Medical Science in the Leatherwoods

Among my earliest recollections are those of doctors and medicines. When I was a very small boy, my elders impressed upon me the fact that doctors are almost unerring guides in mortal welfare, and that medicines, especially patent medicines, work miracles in preserving and restoring health. So profound and unshakable were these early impressions that they have stayed with me through the years even down to the present hour. Through my liberal patronage during the last fifty years, more than one small-town doctor has been able to provide himself with luxuries, and several druggists have turned my purchases into dividends and taken long vacation tours. I attribute my hale and hearty condition as I write these reminiscences to my insight in recognizing the merits of doctors, prescriptions, and patent medicines. Upon the appearance of the slightest symptom of physical disorder I send for a doctor and supplement his treatments and prescriptions with liberal quantities of good patent and proprietary medicines. I recommend this practice to my friends.

Most of the country doctors in the Leatherwood Mountains in the 1870s were innocent of any contacts with medical colleges. Their knowledge of anatomy and disease was acquired by main strength and awkwardness, and their mistakes, fortunately, were not mentioned on the tombstones of their patients. There were no local or state medical boards or other regulatory bodies to investigate their knowledge and proficiency, and they were not forced to stand examination in order to get a license to practice. The qualifications for the title of Doctor and all privileges appertaining thereunto were remarkably simple: an aspirant to the profession needed only a pair of pill-bags and a crop of whiskers.

In those days a beard was considered prima facie evidence of wisdom, medical expertness, and long experience. One of the greatest struggles of the young doctors was to grow a good crop of whiskers—especially side-burns—always a sign of wisdom and professional competence.

I vividly recall the visits of the country doctor. He rode a good horse and carried across his saddle a pair of square-looking, double-decked containers called by the euphonious name of "pill-bags." He strode into the sick-room, grave, dignified, bewhiskered, amid the hushed admiration of the whole family. He began his examination by looking at the patient's tongue and completed it by feeling his pulse and asking a few questions. With this information, his grasp of the situation was complete. He needed nothing else. His course was clear. His understanding of the case was not beclouded with laboratory data, and he enjoyed the additional advantage of never having heard of more than a few score of the thousands of diseases now known to medical science. The remedy he prescribed was simple, and his instructions were easily followed.

He sat with his pill-bag across his knees and took out various small bottles of different colored powders. After cutting up a number of little squares of paper with his penknife, he would open one of the bottles and take out on his pocketknife blade a small portion of, let us say, white powders, and deposit the proper amount on each of the little squares of paper. Next he would open a bottle of brown powders and repeat the performance with his knife blade. Then, perhaps, he would open a third bottle, this time of yellow powders, and add a small quantity of it to each of the papers on the table before him. And finally he would fold these slips of paper very neatly and give instructions about doses. Occasionally he left a small bottle of "drops" of some kind to be given between the doses of powders. And he always prescribed two large drastic "blue-mass" pills,* about the size of partridge eggs, to be taken first.

Meanwhile, members of the family stood about in open-eyed wonder and admiration at his amazing accuracy in diagnosing the case and prescribing the remedy. None of us ever dreamed of ques-

---

*A strong purgative, these pills were made by combining quicksilver with confection of roses.

tioning the diagnosis. As for me, I felt that the end of all medical knowledge sat before me.

Our family doctor was Thomas B. Morton, one of Baxter County's best citizens. He was tall and square, a picturesque figure, with an impressive iron-gray beard that came to a blunt point some distance below his chin. No one who knew him ever doubted his honesty and sincerity. And his patients believed firmly in his prescriptions, even though they might occasionally quail before the rigor of his treatments.

One winter day Uncle sent for him after he had been wrestling for a week with a severe attack of biliousness. He and Dr. Morton were long-time neighbors and the best of friends. After making such examination of my uncle as he thought necessary, the Doctor prescribed the customary dose of two large blue-mass pills. Mr. Swan was well acquainted with the virtues of those pills, and he held them in mortal dread. The more he thought about them, the more he was inclined to consider the remedy worse than the disease, and he finally decided to take his chances of getting well without their help.

Ten days later Dr. Morton was called into our neighborhood and rode two miles out of his way to come and see how Mr. Swan was doing. When he stepped in and saw my uncle sitting by the fireside, looking much better than on his previous visit, he exclaimed in his usual loud voice, "Well, William, I'm powerful glad to see you looking so well. I thought them pills would bring you 'round all right."

Mr. Swan was a very sincere, conscientious man who never sailed under false colors. After looking into the fire for two full minutes, he turned to Dr. Morton with a rather sheepish look on his face and said, "Doc, I didn't take them pills."

Dr. Morton, in turn, looked steadily into the fire for some time. Then he looked up and said, "Well, William, I think they'd 'a' done you good."

As far as my knowledge goes, all the doctors back in the Leatherwood Mountains were conscientious men of plain, practical sense and high moral character. No doubt each of them owned a book or two, like Gunn's *Domestic Medicine*, and studied them until they knew the simple remedies for simple diseases. Perhaps their greatest assets as doctors were their firm belief in the sacredness of human life and an interest in their patients that was personal and genuine. Had they been unscrupulous men taking advantage of the lack of professional regulation, our woes would have been greatly multiplied.

If doctors were scarce in the Leatherwood Mountains, so were diseases. Few of us would have survived if we had had to run the gamut of all the ills that now lie in wait along life's pathway. There was no such thing, for instance, as blood pressure, either high or low, and consequently we were not frightened out of our wits every few months by the doctor telling us that our blood pressure was so high it was likely to burst every vein in our immortal bodies, or that it was so low we were liable to lapse into a coma right in the midst of our plans for covering the barn. We did not have appendixes; influenza had not been discovered; cirrhosis of the liver was unknown to us; tonsilitis had not been heard of (but there was a "right smart sore throat" in the neighborhood). Arthritis, osteitis, sciatica, arteriosclerosis, osteomyelitis, conjunctivitis, peritonitis, floating kidney, thrombosis, and ten thousand other diseases that have been corralled, branded, and turned loose on humanity by the medical profession did not have to be reckoned with.

The scarcity of doctors in the backwoods made it necessary for the heads of families to do much of the doctoring within the family circle. As a matter of fact, ordinary sickness was not taken too seriously in our community, unless the man of the house was the patient, in which case he would grunt and groan like a horse with the colic, and would have everyone on the place waiting on him, while one member of the family was sent, post haste, for the doctor. At least such was the case with one or two of our neighbors. If the wife or the children got sick, it was nothing serious and they would be well in a day or two—no use to go to the expense of sending for the doctor.

In the backwoods, folks spoke their minds freely, pretty unconcerned about the tact and etiquette that townpeople expect. Years after I left the Leatherwoods I learned this story about how Aunt comforted a sick relative, who was recovering from a serious attack of typhoid fever. She asked the usual question, and the patient told her that the worst was over and he felt well, so well that he expected to be up in a few days. She replied, "Well, you can't always tell by your feelings. I remember when John Teague had typhoid, he looked just about like you do and said the crisis was over and he would be up in a few days, but he was a dead man in twelve hours."

In most cases of illness the housewives were the doctors, and the majority of them were medical-minded and economy-wise. They had by rote a hundred or two old remedies, handed down by tradition from past generations or learned from the Indians, and they used these remedies with great confidence, supplementing them with patent medicines. For their drugs they depended mainly upon the "yarb" (herb) garden and the forest. My aunt took great pride in her yarbs, and with reason, for she had a wide variety of them. There were peppermint, catnip, sage, senna, thyme, rue, horehound, sweet basil, wormwood, horseradish, golden seal, calamus, horsemint, pennyroyal, sweet fennel, anise root, Virginia snakeroot, and doubtless others that I have forgotten. One of the lingering delights of the herb garden is the recollection of the fragrance of many of these plants. Crushing the leaves brings out the odors of such herbs as basil, catnip, balm, marjoram, dill, and sweet fennel; and the dried leaves and roots of others yield an aroma that carries me back to the Leatherwoods: sage, coriander, rosemary, thyme, caraway, and lavender in particular remain vividly with me. The following additional plants, shrubs, and trees all grew wild and furnished the ingredients for many other remedies: slippery elm, wild cherry, wild plum, wahoo, spicewood, white oak, mullein, sumac, sassafack (sassafras), ginseng, yellow dock, burdock, plantain, Jerusalem oak, tansy, May apple, rattlesnake master, yellow puccoon, and prickly pear. Against such an array of medical yarbs, barks, and roots, the ordinary ailment did not have a sporting chance.

Did the baby have the colic, croup, or hives? Calamus root, senna tea, Jerusalem oak mixed with honey, sassafras bark tea—one or all—would bring quick relief. Rheumatism had very little chance to get anywhere when promptly treated with a mixture of wahoo bark, wild cherry bark bitters, and Virginia snakeroot. For coughs and colds nothing could take the place of a gallon or two of a compound made up of burdock root, wild cherry, prickly ash bark, sarsaparilla, horehound, and honey. The dose was a teacupful four times a day. For eye irritations we were advised to get a thick leaf of prickly pear, burn off the spines, rub off the small brown stickers, and roast it in hot ashes. Then split it in two, place a half over each eye, cut side down, and tie in place at bed time. The next morning all the irritation would be gone. This remedy was equally effective in the treatment of boils. Biliousness was very common, but it was easily conquered by frequent doses of a tonic made of whiskey, wild cherry bark, burdock root, and buck tansy, taken in liberal quantities. This tonic was also a splendid blood purifier. For general debility, Virginia snakeroot was a specific. Soreness in any part of the body was quickly cured with goose grease. Mutton "taller" relieved chapped hands or lips. To thicken the blood, golden seal salve, blood root and Indian turnip seasoned in whiskey, and sassafras tea were standard medicines. Some of the old women of the neighborhood believed firmly that sassafras root tea purified the blood while making it thick, whereas others insisted that spicewood tea promoted good health by thinning the blood. Our family had faith in both of these tonics and used them in the belief that our blood was in occasional need of thickening or thinning, either or both, but we could never recall, when we were taking one of the teas, what was being done to us. Was our blood becoming watery or gummy? We never knew, but after we finished the course we always felt much better. Slippery elm was one of the most useful of all the medicinal plants. When soaked in water it produced a thick slime, which was used to cover quinine in the eternal but vain hope that the dose would slip down untasted. Elm was also used in poultices. For pleurisy pains, a plaster as big as a saddle blanket was coated with ground mustard, flour, and vinegar and applied to the chest. It was worse than the pains.

I will never forget the time I had a severe pain in my side and the doctor prescribed one of these vinegar-mustard poultices. It was duly applied, but in three minutes or less it was burning me up. I threw it off and had a thickness of cloth put next to my skin and the poultice replaced. Off it came again in a moment, and I inserted three thicknesses of cloth and once more put it back. But it was no use—I couldn't stand it. Finally I got a piece of leather and slipped it under the poultice. It had the desired effect, and I was soon asleep and the next morning entirely well.

There was no tuberculosis back in the mountains. Consumption was rather common, and it was treated according to the latest methods of medical science. In cold weather the patient was made to wear warm, heavy clothing, and was kept in the warmest and most nearly air-tight room on the place lest a blast of fresh, cold air strike him and give him a chill or a fresh cold. He was never permitted to go out of doors, but was kept close to a warm fire, day and night. In late spring and summer, he was encouraged to take plenty of exercise and chop wood, hoe cotton, and walk as far and as often as his strength permitted. Consumption was frequently fatal in those days.

Some of the older women of the neighborhood used "charms" to cure certain afflictions. My aunt was one of them—she had a "charm" for burns. If anyone got badly burned, she would be sent for, since her reputation as a successful healer was rather extensive. Not a year passed without someone's getting burned, and Aunt's ministrations were always preferred to the doctor's. We never knew the details of her treatment—they remained a profound secret, and her patients would not talk much about what she did. When she came home from a visit to a patient—she never had to give more than one treatment to each patient—she would still be wrapped in an air of mystery, and no one asked her any questions. I have heard that she mumbled some sort of incantation learned from the Indians, as she waved her hand over the burn and blew upon it. She believed firmly in her ability to charm the fire out of any ordinary burn, and if she made any failures, no one seemed to be the wiser. Her ability was recognized throughout the City Rock neighborhood as long as she lived.

If I were wealthy, I would build and maintain at my expense memorials in honor of the men who gave to humanity those two great blessings, capsules and sugar-coated pills. It is surprising that some fitting international celebration was not held in their honor long ago. In the early days of which I write, capsules had not been invented, and sugar-coated pills were just beginning to penetrate those outposts of civilization. We had to take our medicines "raw." There were no more sinister threats to household peace than the old-fashioned un-coated pills. Old-timers will recall what an appalling flavor they had. Even the sight of the little oval box with the small gray pills filled us with dread and gloom. Children looked upon them with horror and loathing and wrath. Right well do I remember the first sugar-coated pill I ever took, so white and sweet. I thought it was sugar-coated all the way through, so I stole two out of the box when the folks were not looking and chewed them up. Verily life is full of surprises and dis-appointments, and these begin right early.

Among those who lived on the river, third-day chills were a popular pastime, caused by breathing the fog and the foul air of the lowlands. Every family kept constantly on hand a liberal supply of quinine, which was taken regularly. There being no capsules, it had to be taken raw—or even worse. A wide-spread notion was that quinine taken in cold coffee was not disagreeable. I have tried it that way, and it remains one of life's unsolved mysteries how anyone ever believed that cold coffee does anything but aggravate the bitter taste of quinine. Another strategem to make it less disagreeable was to wrap up the dose in cooked dried peaches. The roll made was as large as a pullet egg, and the victim would undertake to swallow it whole. But the peach would invariably burst, and then the quinine would get in its malignant work on the taste buds.

The deep and lasting impression made on my youthful mind by medicines did not grow altogether out of the experiences already al-luded to. I think my most vivid impression and the one most indelibly stamped on my memory, grew out of the set-to with my aunt and uncle when Saturday night came and the weekly dosage of castor oil had to be administered to the children, regardless of their physical condition. To each tablespoonful of this delightful nectar a few drops of turpentine were added to give it zest and tone. There is no other drug known in *materia medica* that would not improve the taste of castor oil when added to it except turpentine—turpentine makes it worse. We children looked forward to Saturday as a day of execution. When the fatal hour arrived we would protest that we were not sick, that we did not need any castor oil, that we never felt better in our lives, as further evidence of which we would poke out our tongues a few inches to show how well we were. But it was all of no avail—the castor oil had to go down. Some of us would yield to the inevitable with stoical courage, while others would gargle and sputter and strangle and struggle for minutes. To this day the thought of it gives me the shudders.

All my adult life I have had to listen to diatribes and dire warnings against patent medicines. But the advertisements put forth by the men who sell these valuable drugs are so convincing and reassuring that I have given little heed to all pessimistic utterances and gloomy prophecies about them. In youth I drenched my system with Vinegar Bitters, Payne's Celery Compound, Jayne's Expectorant, Warner's Safe Cure, S. S. S., Dr. Harter's Iron Tonic, McLean's Vermifuge, and many other reliable remedies, although I do not remember that I was ever sick at any time. As I have said, my aunt and uncle were great believers in patent medicines and always had a good supply on hand. When winter was over and there would be a few doses left of Wild Cherry Bitters and the other medicines named above, along with the remnants of several of the family doctor's prescriptions for coughs, colds, bronchitis, colic, etc. These would include syrup of squills, sweet spirits of nitre, and cod liver oil. My aunt was a very practical person and did not like to see all this good medicine go to waste. So she would get a large bottle, holding about a quart, pour all these left-over remedies and prescriptions into it, shake it up well, and make us take it as a spring tonic! Those were happy days.

Through rich experience I have learned that in judging medicines of every kind one needs to be broad-minded. To recognize in all of them their true values and health-giving, life-giving virtues is to insure oneself against being carried off by some insidious disease that might slip up on one unawares. Long ago I resolved not to tie myself down to any one or two or half a dozen remedies, so that, if circumstances were such that I was not able to lay my hands on a favorite remedy, I could get along just as well by adapting myself to almost any other kind of medicine that was available. Or if I had used up the supply of my favorite cure, I could then try a bottle of something else, and usually it worked quite as well as the other, if not better. I make a practice of reading the newspapers closely to learn about new remedies for any disease new or old, and as soon as the local drugstores lay in a supply, I buy a bottle in the expectation that some time it will come in handy. If the local druggist does not act promptly, I become impatient and order direct from the manufacturer. Fortified by my stock of patent and proprietary medicines and drugs, I feel secure against attack. I do not take all these, to be sure, any more than I take all of the doctor's prescriptions, but I like to have them sitting on my shelves. They give me a feeling of confidence that is worth more than gold and silver.

From experience I have also learned that even horse medicine is a health-giving drug, and on occasion can be taken to great advantage. Several years ago I attended a picnic dinner in the country where the food was served in abundance on a long row of makeshift tables. I was unusually hungry and ate generously of practically everything spread before me. My friend and companion, Watt Moore, was just as hungry. We began at one end of the row of tables and ate our way down to the other end, turned the corner and came on back, eating heartily all the way. There was lots of barbecued mutton, some of it well cooked, some fairly well cooked, and some rather rare. We began on the mutton. Fried chicken came next. Then fried ham, pickles, hard-boiled eggs, cabbage, sausage, jelly, kraut, fried pies, cake of several kinds, and peach cobbler.

We were sent to the home of a farmer in the community to stay all night. Far in the night—about one-thirty—my slumbers were rudely broken by a keen pain, as sharp as a dagger, piercing me amid-ships. After the first paralyzing spasm was over, I got out of bed quickly and began to dress. My movements awakened my friend Moore, who inquired what the trouble was. When I told him, he was greatly amused, and his only comment was, "Ha! ha! ha!" He held his sides, he roared, he rolled with laughter. Then the laughter suddenly ceased, he sat up in bed, looked wildly out of his eyes, and an expression of agony took the place of his grin. "Hold on," he said as I was hurrying out of the room; "I'll go with you." A terrible pain had struck him, he explained. It felt like a butcher-knife being plunged into his vitals. He got up and began to dress hurriedly.

After the third attack an hour later, we awakened our host, told him of the calamitous times that were upon us, and asked if he had any medicine on the place. He said there was not a drop of any kind except a quart bottle of horse medicine which he had found useful when his horses had the colic. "Let me see it!" I said. By the light of a dim, greasy coal-oil lamp, my eyes were gladdened by the sight of this legend: "Good For Man Or Beast." I asked him for a teacup, poured it half full, and drank it down, every drop of it. I poured the teacup half full again and offered it to Moore. I had some doubts about his acceptance of my kindly offer, but he grasped the cup eagerly and took it all at one gulp. In half an hour we were sleeping peacefully, and the next morning we got up feeling as fit as fiddles.

Just how long the itinerant medicine vendor has been traveling about over the country, giving entertainments on the street corners and selling his infallible remedies for all the ills that afflict mankind, such as rheumatism, consumption, dyspepsia, bunions, baldness, cancer, and so on—just how long I do not know. I was nineteen when the first one came up over my horizon. The celebrated artist— unquestionably he was an artist in his line—swept into Mountain Home one midsummer day. His name was Laird—"Dr. Laird," he called himself, since he professed to hold degrees from several of the outstanding medical colleges of the country. He did not exhibit his diplomas, but his audience was quite willing to accept his word.

Dr. Laird gave his first lecture on a street corner, but his instruction was so interesting and illuminating and vital that the Baxter County officials courteously offered him the courtnouse for his entertainment and discourses. The building was packed nightly —everyone went to hear him. He would announce on the street during the day that at night he would devote his first twenty minutes to pulling teeth gratis. He extracted them with his bare fingers, scorning the use of pullicans, and threw the teeth all over the courtroom as he jerked them out. Every snaggle-toothed person for miles around who had the courage came to these free performances and got rid of his bad teeth.

When the tooth-pulling exhibition was over, the doctor would launch out into his lecture, starting with some popular topic, and gradually work around to the practice of medicine, picturing in forceful terms the dangerous condition almost everyone was in without knowing it. He would then describe the apparently trivial but really alarming symptoms of these terrible maladies that were undermining the constitution of nearly every man, woman, and child within the

sound of his voice. He told us plainly that these symptoms, to which little attention is ordinarily given, even by those who think they are in good health, were in reality sign-posts, showing plainly that persons having any of them were headed for the grave, and that right early, unless they were fortunate enough to obtain some of the medicine he was selling, of which he had only a few bottles left. Among the terrifying symptoms he mentioned as indicating the approaching crisis of some dread disease in its last stage, I recall a few: rapid beating of the heart after taking exercise; shortness of breath after climbing ladders or running up steps; a feeling of fullness in the stomach after eating; procrastination about getting up on cold mornings; an inclination to eat too much; and an aversion to manual labor. These were all bad symptoms, and he told of many cases in which persons afflicted with them had delayed until they stood on the brink of the grave. Then at last they had discovered his wonderful medicines and had had to take only a few bottles to effect a complete cure.

When I went to the lecture I considered myself in prime physical condition. I had not had an ache or pain for years, except growing pains. But before the lecture was fifteen minutes old I was becoming worried about my health, which had begun to deteriorate rapidly; a half-hour more, and I had lost all hope. But as Dr. Laird began to recount the numerous cures which he had effected, I saw that I had one chance to live. And before he concluded, I was convinced that what I needed most in this world was his medicine—and lots of it—immediately. I did not quite have the courage to stand up in the crowd and buy a bottle of his elixir of life, but after the entertainment was over, I followed him to his "hotel" and asked a private audience with him, which he graciously granted. By a few well-directed questions he ascertained that mine was no ordinary case, to be treated in an ordinary way, but that it needed special handling, and he went out of his way to accommodate me by giving me a special prescription. He took a quart bottle and with scientific accuracy poured into it several different kinds of his life-giving drugs until the bottle was full. He charged me only two dollars for it, which was almost like giving it away, since he had furnished the special prescription and the medicine, as well as the bottle. I deeply appreciated such generosity from a total stranger, and could hardly find words to express my gratitude. He assured me that if I would take the remedy three times a day I would have a fighting chance to overcome the diseases that were so rapidly undermining my health. I hastened to my room in order to lose no time in beginning the treatment, gulped down a dose, and went to bed. That was the only dose I ever took. It isn't often that one dose effects a complete cure, especially when the malady has such a strangle hold on one's vitals, but by morning the spell cast over me by Dr. Laird had vanished, and along with it my ills.

The traveling medicine vendor survived far into the twentieth century. We saw him every year in the upper White River towns of the Ozark country, dispensing his precious remedies to a grateful population.

Chapter VIII
Social Life

Among the settlers in the Leatherwood Mountains in the 1870s hospitality was a very common virtue and a very genuine one, but it was very different from the hospitality of the Old South in that it was utterly unselfconscious and informal to the last degree. To the White River folks it was not an obligation or a matter of etiquette. It sprang wholly from goodness of heart and a spirit of neighborliness—and the neighbor might be a member of the nearest family a mile or two away, or a total stranger. There was no formality about making or "returning" calls: folks went to see one another when they wanted to, never out of politeness, and were as likely to drop in at dinner time as at any other hour of the day. It was customary to invite visitors to spend the night. "You'ens stay all night with us" was as often heard as "Come on in and set down." The people of the Leatherwoods never charged travelers for meals and a bed. In fact, strangers coming through the country were warmly welcomed, especially if they were intelligent and knew how to respond to backwoods hospitality.

Late one October afternoon in 1877, shortly after I went to live with the Swans, a memorable event took place in our household. An agent for the Southern Clock Company appeared at our door, having managed somehow to drive his two-horse vehicle over our so-called roads. He spent the night with us, and the next morning he unboxed and set up one of his calendar clocks. It was about as tall as the old-fashioned Seth Thomas weight clocks, but hardly as wide, and was strongly built of black walnut and handsomely finished. The face of the clock showed not only the minutes and hours but also the day of the week, the day of the month, and the year. Every four years it

101

would show February with twenty-nine days instead of twenty-eight. The agent did not get an opportunity to use all of his spiel about the many virtues of the clock, so eager were all the family to close the trade. He demonstrated the strength of the clock by bearing his weight on it, and the sale was made. The price was $33.33, which Uncle paid in cash. The family watched the clock most of that day and sat up until midnight several times to see the automatic changes take place in the day of the week and the month. News of this remarkable clock soon spread through the community, and for the next six months visitors came from miles around to sit and watch it for a few hours and have its wonders explained to them. More than a few remained overnight to watch the jump at midnight from one day to the next.

One might be disposed to think that our backwoods cabin, a hundred miles from railroad and telegraph office, having home-made furnishings and a library of three books, would be avoided by travelers looking for comfortable lodging, congenial entertainment, or aid in time of need. But that would be an erroneous conclusion, for our home was known to be supplied with all that was necessary for contented, comfortable rural living. The house was of double-log construction,* with eighty acres of pleasant surrounding land and as cold a spring pouring from under the mountain side as I have ever seen. Again I must make mention of the "board" at the Swans' with all the sweets mortal could wish for—jellies and jams, honey, canned and preserved fruit; vegetables from the garden or the ground storage, where they had been "holded up" since the growing season; a plentiful supply of meats, milk, and butter. The traveler who rode up to the gate out in front of the Swan home about supper time and had borne out to his nostrils on the evening breeze the aroma of country ham and black gravy frying in the fireplace or on the kitchen stove would be very reluctant to push farther on that night. For me that home-cured ham and black gravy have lingering attractions. A few people still living recall that travelers going through the White River country from Batesville to the cedar forests and zinc fields of Marion and southern Baxter Counties would pace themselves so as to reach the home of the Swans in time to spend the night. Its reputation for good country food and comfortable feather beds reached far beyond county lines. Having once stopped here, travelers could be expected to favor us with other visits whenever business called them through the

*That is, it was two houses with a breezeway between.

Leatherwoods. Sometimes this reputation was a disadvantage to the Swans, as we shall see.

Walton and I contributed to the entertainment of visitors by getting out the last issue of *Farm and Home* and asking them to read it to us, while we sat and listened intently, just as though we did not know its contents almost by heart. We watched all visitors closely, listened eagerly, and talked over what they said for days afterwards.

Occasionally, when the strangers were not used to backwoods ways, they made mis-steps of various kinds. Once a Mr. Bob Hurst and his assistant were surveying in our section and staying for a day or two with our neighbor, Mr. Emory. At their first meal Mrs. Emory asked them whether they would have long or short sweetening in their coffee. Neither of them had any notion of what the "long" or "short" might be, but they did not want to appear ignorant, so Mr. Hurst said that he would take long sweetening; whereupon Mrs. Emory poured about two tablespoonfuls of molasses into his coffee. Seeing this, his assistant at once asked for short sweetening. Of course he was not sure what it was, but he was ready to take a chance rather than have his coffee spoiled with molasses. He was relieved to see Mrs. Emory put sugar in his coffee. Mr. Hurst made the best of the situation and drank his molasses-sweetened coffee with seeming relish, as though he had been raised on long sweetening. At breakfast the next morning he had decided that he would call for short sweetening, but Mrs. Emory remembered his preference and, before he had a chance to speak, liberally sweetened his coffee with molasses. His assistant chuckled all that day over Mr. Hurst's hard luck.

Usually, however, when guests were entertained, the disadvantages were with the hosts, not with the guests. A church was only a short distance from the Swan home, and once a month services were held, attended by perhaps a hundred people. On such occasions I have seen thirty invite themselves to dinner at the Swans'. Hospitality in the Leatherwood Mountains was informal, as I have already said. There were some neighbors living twelve miles away, in another county, who had no vehicle and no horses or mules, but who felt strongly the urge to attend these monthly services of the little backwoods church, of which they were not members, although it involved a walk of twenty-four miles for the round trip. Their explanation was that they were needed to lead the singing. But the explanation was a flimsy one—they were very poor singers, and even if they had been good, they would have found it humanly impossible to lead the kind of singing we had. In order not to miss any part of the possible preliminary services, these men, three in number, would come to our house on Friday afternoons and remain until Monday mornings, thus connecting up with the services in general and with the sustenance in particular. Their appetites, whetted to a keen edge by the twelve-mile walk, responded very favorably to the good food that the Swan table offered. They rewarded the Swans for their hospitality by singing loud and long, morning, noon, and night. In fact, they were singing most of the time they weren't eating. When the weather was bad and we did not expect many at church—not even the preacher himself if the weather was cold and raw—we could always count on the steadfast loyalty of these three neighbors from across the River—in spite of rain or snow or storm. They were very religious. If Aunt and Uncle ever grew weary of extending hospitality to a never-ending procession of guests, including the three singers, no one heard them utter a murmur of complaint. They took it for granted, as did all the people of the backwoods, that their home was always open to a neighbor, just as it was accepted that every one helped a neighbor with his farming or his building.

Of course there were exceptions, and one case of reluctant hospitality that took place before I went to live with the Swans made a lasting impression on me. Mr. and Mrs. William Hixson, rugged and prosperous, were our nearest neighbors. Mrs. Hixson, who was low and wide and fat, and known to everyone as "Aunt Polly," prided herself on her really good German cooking, and on occasion she loved to have her neighbors sample her dishes. Her masterpiece was a certain apple pie, which she called by its German name. As well as I can remember, she called it something that sounded like "Ep-i-kish-el."* When she had built up one of these pies and put on the finishing touches it was a work of art. One Sunday she invited my mother and sister and me to have dinner with them. Sitting in the front room with Mr. Hixson, I knew one of those pies was coming up and waited impatiently for the dinner hour to arrive. About eleven-thirty in walked Mr. Plunk, a shiftless tenant from a neighboring farm two miles away. He had brought along with him an equally shiftless and hungry neighbor. Aunt Polly knew they had invited themselves for no other purpose than to fill up on her Sunday dinner, and she was wroth. She fussed and fumed around the kitchen, talking pretty loud to my mother about folks who would leave their wives and children at home

*Apfel Kissen, pronounced "apfel kishen" in South Germany, is an apple tart made with a yeast dough rather than a pastry crust.

with nothing to eat but cornbread and bacon, while they walked off and sponged on their neighbors for Sunday dinners. These remarks fell on deaf ears, however, for Mr. Plunk and his friend politely took no notice of them. Presently "Aunt Polly" came to the door and announced, more or less diplomatically: "Hixson, you and John come on in to dinner; I reckon the others has been to dinner." Instantly Mr. Plunk was on his feet with a disclaimer: "No'm we hain't," he said, and he and his friend walked right in to the table, took seats, and ate as heartily as if they were guests of honor. They held no narrow views of hospitality. And by passing their plates for second and third helpings, they showed so clearly their entire satisfaction with the dinner that they did not find it necessary to thank Mrs. Hixson or compliment her on her cooking. Hospitality in the Ozarks was *very* informal.

The Leatherwoods people had a special liking for two or three kinds of humor. Dry humor was second nature with them, as their manner of living prompted hard-bitten, reserved expressions. "Sev'ral" meant "a good many," "a leetle" meant "a good bit," and "right smart" meant "very." And from a visitor at our home in Calico Rock before I lived with the Swans I learned some arithmetic not found in the books. A visitor, Mr. Tom Stallings, asked me if I would bring him "two-or-three" persimmons from the yard. As I was only six years old and had never heard the expression before, I did not know how many "two-or-three" was. Was it two? was it three? or two and a half? After some hesitation under the tree I picked up three persimmons, deciding to take my chances on guessing what he wanted. He accepted all three, and then I knew that I had made a discovery—I had learned that "two-or-three" meant three, that whenever anyone asked for "two-or-three," he wanted three, and it was proper to give him three. I was pleased with my discovery, and in the seventy years that have passed since then I have had no reason to revise my figures.

Sayings of local origin were another form of humor, and the hills were full of them. Examples: "Shoot, Luke, or give up the gun"; and "Every man thinks his own dirt's clean." Tall tales like "The Split Dog," "The Three Wishes," and "The Six Irishmen Who Couldn't Count" were told and re-told until every one knew them. The favorite stories, however, were events that happened in the hills, and among these were many amusing ones. The following story about Lem Tinnin, which was told through several generations or as long as Lem was remembered, is typical. Big camp meetings were held late every summer across the River near North Fork. Farmers and their families would come from far-away in their wagons and stay through the two weeks of the meeting. Some of the farmers would bring fresh cider to sell, and their wives would bake large ginger cakes to sell along with the cider. One day Az Tinnin was sitting in the meeting with his two boys, Jake and Lem. Lem was only four years old, and before the sermon was over he was getting pretty hungry. So he whispered to his father to get him a ginger cake. Az told him he would after a while. But Lem was not to be put off so easily and he continued to ask his pa for the ginger cake, getting louder and louder and more and more insistent. At length he began whimpering and crying until everyone in the brush arbor was more interested in the ginger cake than in the sermon. Eventually Az got his fill of Lem and, getting a dime out of his pocket, gave it to Jake and told him to get the cake in a hurry. When Jake was almost out of the brush arbor, Lem rose up and yelled to his brother, "Jake, git a big un," and the whole congregation broke out in loud laughter. For a half century this story drew a laugh whenever it was told, or even whenever someone quoted, "Jake, git a big un."

In these latter days the practical joker has fallen from grace. He is generally looked upon as a nuisance, or worse, one who has his fun at the expense of others. But back in the Ozark villages during the eighties and nineties and even later, he was appreciated as a man who livened things up in his community. His jokes, played among his close friends and acquaintances, were of such a kind that the victims could usually enjoy them as much—or almost as much—as the rest of the village. Practical joking was common practice, as most of the leading citizens did a good deal of it, and nearly every town and village had their prime jokesters, who were topics of conversation and pride in the communities.

The best and most dedicated practical joker I have known was Lee Paul, of Mountain Home, a small village not far from my native hills. Mr. Paul, a master jokester, would go to no end of trouble to make sure that his pranks came off well. Among his many jokes my favorite is the one he perpetrated on the Methodist brethren of the village at Conference time.

The two-day Conference was dated to begin at Mountain Home on a Thursday, and the brethren from two or three counties were expected to attend. On Monday, three days before the opening session of the Conference, Paul borrowed a covered wagon and a team of mules and got Vin Truman to dress as a woman who posed as his wife. The two of them set out about bed-time on their excursion and called on the most prominent Methodists of the village. Their first stop was at the William Hailey residence, where Paul knocked at the door. Hailey answered his knock, and disguising his voice Paul announced from the darkness: "I'm Reverend Silas Hicks, from Lead Hill, and this is my wife. We've come down to attend the Conference this week. We came a little ahead of time because we need to rest and eat and sleep a few days so's to be in good shape to take in the Conference. The Committee wrote us that we were going to be entertained in your home, and we're ready to move in."

The good Methodist brother began to protest: "Why, the Committee never said a word to me about any guests, so I'm not prepared for you yet."

Paul replied, "Well, the Committee certainly gave us your name as our host, and we've come a long way. We're tired and hungry and our three little children are all worn out. But a bite to eat and a good night's sleep is all it'll take to fix us up. We were sure you would welcome us fellow Methodists at your house."

"Brother Hicks, I'm pleased that you are here for the Conference, and I'd like to have you stay with me, but I've got three roomers here and haven't got a place in the house where I could put any visitors."

"Now don't you worry about that," answered Paul. "All we need for tonight is a floor to sleep on and a couple of quilts. You've sure got that. A crust of bread, so to speak, will take care of our needs for tonight."

"But I tell you I haven't got a place to put you. Every room in the house is full, and I ain't got anything to eat."

Believing that he had gone far enough, Lee asked for a drink of fresh water from the well, and inquired whether Hailey thought Sam Livingston, down the street, might have room for them.

"He might," replied Hailey, pleased at the thought of getting rid of his unwelcome visitors. He drew a bucket of water from the well, gave them a drink, wished them luck in finding lodging for the evening, and told them goodnight.

Well pleased with the prevarications they had drawn out of their friend Hailey, Paul and Truman proceeded to the home of Brother Livingston, and after rousing him Paul announced, "Me and my wife and four children has drove in from Marion County to attend the Conference. We come early as we allus do so's to have more fellership with the brothern. Mr. Hailey told us we was to come to your house.

We're jist plain country folks—don't expect nothin' fancy to eat—jist plenty of good plain vittles—"

Brother Livingston interrupted: "Hailey must have made a mistake. Uh—you see—two of my children are mighty sick with the measles, and it looks like the other one may have whoopin' cough."

Lee replied, "Now, don't let that bother you none, Brother Livingston. My young uns has all had whoopin' cough and two kinds of measles. We kin help take keer of the sick fer ye."

"But," said Livingston, "there's been a mistake. We're supposed to keep three men during the Conference, and they might come in tonight, and if they did, we'd be in a bad mix-up."

Lee asked for a drink of cold water, which Brother Livingston drew from the well without enthusiasm, and then he and Vin continued their rounds.

At the next house Bob Hancock told Lee and Vin that his wife was visiting in Texas and that he had no way to feed any visitors.

"Now, don't you worry about that a minute," replied Paul. "My wife is as good a cook as you can find, and she can just take over your house and cook all the food we can eat. You'll be doin' yourself a favor as well as us by takin' us in."

"Bu—but you see, my wife's comin' home tomorrow and she's bringin' her sister and the whole family back with her for a visit."

Lee and Vin left after getting Hancock to draw a bucket of water from the well for them.

At the home of John Shipp, who greeted the visitors in his night clothes, Paul began:

"We're the Hickses, just drove in for the Conference. This is my wife, and my five children is out there in the wagon. The Committee wrote us that you was to keep us durin' the meetin'. We're mighty tired, and two of the children is ailin'. The baby's fretful, been cryin' all day. But we know that you're the good Samaritan that'll take us in."

"Ah—Brother Hicks, we'd like to have you stay with us, but we just got word this evenin' that my Uncle Joe, over in Fulton County, died last night, and the whole family is leavin' at sunrise for the funeral."

"Never mind that," said Paul. "We'll be glad to keep house fer ye till you git back."

"Ah—couldn't do that," said Shipp. "We're clean out of meat and corn meal. I was aimin' to go over to my brother's early tomorrow for some meat, and some flour on the way home, but I won't have time. Besides, we ain't sure when we're comin' back after the funeral."

Lee and Vin kept up their rounds till after midnight, crowding their friends into the most clumsy falsehoods. They got an astonishing amount of information about shortages of food, illnesses of various members of the families, carpenters starting the next morning for several days' work on the house, the expected arrival of visitors, news just received calling the whole family away from town, promises already made to entertain three preachers who were coming early to the Conference, and the like.

The next day the whole village was laughing about the Hicksses' early arrival for the Conference and the desperate excuses given them by the Methodist brethren for not taking them in. Even the victims joined in the joking and more or less willingly forgave Paúl —doubtless because each one felt that his neighbor had told a lie as big as his own—or even bigger. Also because such doings were expected from Lee Paul.

For years this story and many others about Lee's jokes were as familiar to the people of Mountain Home as the stories in the McGuffey readers. Probably some of them are still in circulation there.

Our religious services must have been like those held all over the frontier during the nineteenth century. When I was a small boy there were no church houses in our neighborhood but we had preaching once a month in some family residence, turn about. Later two church houses were built, and preaching was held once a month and "protracted meetings" once a year—during the summer—sometimes in brush arbors close to the churches. The sermons were long and tedious, and the singing almost beyond belief. Since we had no song books, someone, usually the preacher's wife, lined out the songs, two lines at a time, like this:

> Amazing grace, how sweet the sound
> That saved a wretch like me.

The congregation would sing these two lines after a fashion, and the leader would line out the next two:

> I once was lost but now am found,
> Was blind but now I see.

Everyone who could sing would join in—and quite a few who couldn't.

Now and then some stranger came into the Leatherwoods and announced a singing school, at a dollar a head for two weeks' instruction. He would get ten or twenty more-or-less apt pupils of all ages. At the beginning of each lesson he would line them all up in a row and extend his right hand toward the right end of the class. "Do-o-o-o-o," he would sing out, holding the note and carrying his arm slowly the length of the row. As the hand passed, each singer would join in, and when the teacher reached the left end, all would have chimed in and "do-o-o" would be swelling from every throat—or nose. But some of the voices would be pitched high, some low, and he would have to go back over the line and come again until he got everyone in tune —always with noteworthy exceptions. Then waving his arm briskly, he would throw himself and his class into the song selected for execution, flinging do's, re's, and mi's around with enthusiasm. In a class of twenty, three or four tolerable singers might be found, but most of them sang in piping voices that chilled the soul.

There was a good sister in our church who just about the time the preacher was rounding the corner of "Fifthly" in his sermon would utter a scream and leap up and go to shouting. She never failed to shout all over the room and with a finger in our faces to warn each of us to flee from the wrath to come. Then she would subside, allowing the preacher to complete his sermon.

The protracted meetings were well attended, for they gave the people of the whole community their one opportunity of getting together to renew friendships and exchange news and gossip. At these meetings, two or more preachers were always present, and when the one who delivered the sermon of an hour-and-a-half finally finished, he would call on a second preacher to "exhort," and the exhorting would go on for a quarter of an hour. Shouting was free, like salvation, at protracted meetings, and a good many Christians took part in this exercise. Sometimes there would be fifteen or twenty shouting at the same time. The long "mourner's bench" was always located at the front, usually at right angles to the other seats, where those "under conviction" would go to pray and be prayed for and talked to. The story was widely told about a convert at a brush arbor revival who became so emotionally wrought up that he ran from the arbor and climbed up a tree to a height of some fifteen feet, then came down shouting, "I got religion! Oh, I got religion up thar in the tree, and it smelled jist like burnt shucks!"

"Elder" Hilton, as he was called, caused a good many people in north Arkansas to revise their notions about pioneer preachers. He had the well-earned reputation of knowing the value of a dollar as well as he knew the doctrines of his church, and woe was the man who tried to cheat him in a trade. The Reverend J. J. Vest, who held monthly services at our backwoods church, told me this story about Elder Hilton. The two preachers were holding a joint revival near Mountain Home, and one night the good Elder failed to show up when time came for the service to begin, so Brother Vest delayed a few minutes and then started the preliminary exercises without him. After several songs and prayers Elder Hilton still had not appeared, but just before preaching was due to begin he entered the church and took his place on the pulpit. While the congregation was finishing the final notes of a song he leaned over to Brother Vest and said, "There's a hoss outside you can trade for and make twenty-five dollars clear profit in cash."

Several years later when I was attending a meeting of a state denominational board, the matter of appointing a business manager came up. Someone objected that a preacher ought not to be chosen because preachers were not good business men. A member of the board from north Arkansas answered this objection by saying that he had once been of the same opinion, but after he traded horses with Brother Hilton he changed his mind.

So far as I knew, Elder Hilton's sharpness as a trader did no injury to his reputation as a preacher and a pastor.

In the Leatherwood Mountains during the 1870s Christmas was not a holiday and not much of a festival day. More often than otherwise the natives, few in number and far apart, celebrated it by picking cotton, or gathering corn, or mending fences, or cutting wood. My own earliest recollection of Christmas was seeing black marks on the outside of our chimney and being told that a mysterious person called Santa Claus had made these marks with his claws as he climbed down the chimney outside the house—like a bear climbing down a tree. He had entered the house through the chimney and had got the claws of his hands and feet all black with soot, then had got more soot on them as he climed back up inside the chimney, and finally had left the black tracks made by his claws as he climbed down on the outside. While in the house he had found several pairs of stockings hanging around the mantlepiece and in the chimney corners, and he had filled them with red apples and sweet cakes.

Thereafter on every Christmas morning, after first looking into my stockings to see what Santa had left, I hurried outside to see if he had left any black claw-prints on the chimney. And sure enough, he had. As the years passed and I began to hear youngsters a few years older than I make skeptical remarks about Santa Claus, I clinched the argument in his favor by saying that every Christmas morning I had seen the claw-tracks he had left on our chimney. So far as I was concerned, that was the end of the matter.

Candy did not figure in the Christmas offerings of Santa Claus in those days, nor did picture books, toys, red sleds, guns, bicycles, coasters, or toy wagons. There were no family Christmas trees or exchange of gifts. Red apples, raisins, almonds, homemade sweet-cakes, and occasionally a pair of red-top boots made up the whole range of Santa's presents. What more could any child ask or expect?

About the year 1875 a neighbor boy whose parents had probably been trading in Batesville, sixty-five miles away, introduced fire-crackers into our neighborhood, and when I saw and heard him exploding them, I thought that he had discovered the perfect way to celebrate Christmas.

There were no Christmas feasts or parties in the Leatherwoods, but near Calico Rock across the river where the country was more thickly settled, I attended a never-to-be-forgotten party at the home of Mr. Boot Woods. My sister and I were invited and we were so afraid we wouldn't get there on time that we went the day before and spent Christmas Eve as well as Christmas day with our hosts. A good many young people were invited, and all of them came, along with several others who had not been invited. And what a hilarious time we had playing Snap, Trot Charley, and other games. I was eight years old and had never before attended a party. It was cold, snow was on the ground, but the games, the food, and the excitement of a get-together of the young folks made it a holiday to be thought about and talked about for years to come. That was the only Christmas party but one that I ever attended until I was fifteen years old, when I went to Mountain Home, thirty miles away, to go to school.

Prior to the Civil War, there was a custom among the heads of families along the White River near the mouth of Big North Fork, most of them slave-owners, of having their slaves build a big fire in their largest fireplace early Christmas morning and then of letting them "take Christmas" in their own way until the back-log was entirely burned up. The slaves exercised a good deal of ingenuity in selecting green and slow-burning varieties of firewood in order to prolong their Christmas freedom to the utmost. One of them cut a large back-log out of a hackberry tree and immersed it in a creek from March until Christmas day, when he put it in the fireplace, built his fire, and went forth carefree to take his Christmas. He returned late in the evening and found that his water-soaked back-log was not yet half burned, so he again left in high spirits and stayed away all night. When he returned the next morning his back-log was still burning, and once more he started to leave for the purpose of concluding his Christmas celebration. But his master had become suspicious about the unusual longevity of the backlog and plied him with some questions which brought out the story of the log that had reposed for nine months on the bottom of the creek. Whereupon the master proclaimed an official end to Christmas and put Ephraim to work.

It was not until I reached Mountain Home at age fifteen that I learned the true meaning of Christmas. Parties were in high favor there, attended by young and old alike, and I heard a great deal about good fellowship and good will, gift-giving and the practice of making little children happy wherever Christianity had penetrated, the world around.

Chapter IX
Big Doings in the Leatherwoods

Now and then Walton and I were allowed to make short trips out of our immediate neighborhood, which kept our minds beating for a week beforehand and gave us things to talk about for days afterward. Once a year we got to go to a gin whose motive power was an old-time treadmill operated by cattle. This was such a novelty to us that we would get on the treadmill and keep step with the cattle for an hour at a time under the happy belief that we were getting a free ride, whereas we were actually helping the cattle turn the wheel.

Much more important was a never-to-be-forgotten day when a small circus came to Pineville, ten miles away across the river, and Uncle took us to see it. Men and women in tights performed on the trapeze, walked the tight-rope, and did all manner of superhuman stunts the likes of which we had never dreamed of, while a couple of clowns, the first we had ever seen or heard of, kept us laughing the whole afternoon. Even the sight of them was hilarious. It was a great show, a high point in our lives that gave us enough material to compare notes on and discuss and argue about for two or three years, since each of us claimed he had seen a good many daring feats that the other had missed entirely.

I was disappointed, however, in one feature of the show. I had heard folks talk about beating a drum and got the idea that it was a large metallic instrument somewhat like an inverted bell and that some strong-armed man would walk up to it with a maul such as is used in splitting rails and give it half a dozen blows that would set it going; then he would go off and leave it be, to ring and reverberate for the next quarter of an hour. When I saw the drum in action, my high expectations suffered a slump. But the clowns and the acrobats more than made amends. Circuses were as good as a trip to a big steamboat landing, maybe even better.

Log-rollings and house-raisings, which had been a familiar part of frontier life for generations, were on the ebb during my boyhood. I attended two of each, and they were big social occasions, very practical and very enjoyable, that drew people from miles around.

When a settler cleared new ground and saved the best logs for his house, kitchen, barn, or smokehouse, a great deal of brush and a good many scrub logs were always left. Eventually he passed the word to his neighbors that on a certain day he was having a log-rolling, and most of them came with their families, bringing horses or mules, grab hooks, crowbars, and other tools that would be useful. While the women chatted and prepared food and the children who weren't watching the log-rolling played games, the men piled the brush and logs into great head-high heaps for burning.

The house-raisings were even more interesting and required more careful planning than the log-rollings because the work called for greater skill. A date was chosen that suited the skilled workers, and well in advance of the day agreed upon, the logs were cut the right length—some ten or twelve feet, others sixteen feet—and hauled up to the spot where the house was to be raised. Long skids were also prepared to slide the logs into position. When the appointed day came, four men handled the logs, rolled or slid or pried them alongside the house-to-be and four expert choppers stood at the four corners of the house to hew notches in the logs so that they would fit the V's cut in the logs that were already in position.

Chopping is really an art, and not every sturdy long-armed six-footer was good at it. To swing an axe high in the air back over the shoulders and then bring it sharply down at exactly the right place and at the right angle with the right force required an accuracy that came only after years of practice. Most men never gained it.

The choppers at the corners would have the last log notched and ready for the next one to be matched with it by the time the four handlers shoved another log up to them. The rest of the men hewed the bark off the log or, if the house-owner wished, flattened the sides of the logs.

It was a jolly crowd of neighbors who raised the house—jolly because they and their families were together in a big social gathering. They found time to discuss the neighborhood news and gossip, to talk about politics, religion, the high prices at the stores, crop prospects, and the candidates for teaching the new "free" schools in the "dee-stricks"; now and then they told jokes and stories.

Meantime at both log-rollings and house-raisings the women would be preparing dinner for the whole company, talking women's talk all the while. By the time dinner was ready everyone had worked up a good appetite. The dinners that I remember included backbones, hog-jowl, sausage, fried ham, chicken, cabbage, turnips, greens, cornbread, biscuits, preserves, jelly, pumpkin pie, butter, milk, and coffee. Promptly at noon a loud blast that could easily be heard a mile away came from the farm house or the impromptu kitchen. It was a familiar sound that struck the ears of the farmers, but the blast of the dinner-horn was never heard in town. The men dropped their crowbars and hand-spikes and axes and headed for the food. When all were seated, and if no minister were present, the head of the house asked a blessing, and everyone fell upon the food, the men first, as was the custom. After dinner both men and women smoked their pipes for half an hour and then went back to their log-rolling or house raising. Before sundown all the logs would have been rolled and fires would be burning all over the cleared ground, but some heaps might be saved for a square dance or other merrymaking that night. In the case of the house-raisings the building would usually have been finished except for chimney, floor, doors, and table, which the owner would make by himself or with the help of one or two neighbors.

I do not think, as some people have said, that the log-rollings and house-raisings were work-swapping deals, day for day. At least in our neighborhood, settlers who had lived on farms where all the land had long since been cleared and all the needed houses built were just as active in the gatherings as were the newcomers. Of course there was a very practical side to the work, but the claims of neighborliness were strong, and the pleasures of a community get-together were genuine. The men and women had good times at these log-rollings and house-raisings; the burden of work was lightened by the enjoyment of friends working together; the food was special; and the feeling of helping a neighbor warmed the heart. The people of the community did not get together often—not nearly often enough. There should have been more of these log-rollings and house-raisings, or if the need for them no longer existed, occasional clear-ups, clean-ups, or some other substitute should have been made.

They were big events in the Leatherwoods—to be remembered
pleasantly for a life-time.

Weddings were so few in the Leatherwoods that they were big
doin's, even to growing boys. So when Mr. Priddy rode about the
neighborhood announcing that his only daughter was to be married
and invited his friends to come to the wedding and the dinner that he
was going to give in honor of the event, Walton and I took notice and
laid plans to attend, notwithstanding the fact that we had not been
invited. I had seen only one wedding, and Walton none, so nothing
could have kept us away from the wedding of Miss Priddy. As the
groom-to-be was Mr. Merrill, a young merchant out in the hills, with
a fifty-dollar stock of goods, Mr. Priddy was much pleased with the
match.

The Priddy home was four miles away from us, but what was an
eight-mile walk to a pair of healthy boys when they could see such a
rare event and maybe get something to eat that was unusual? We were
rewarded for our walk but hardly in the manner expected. We saw
Squire Blount ride up on his horse and enter the crowded house; we
slipped in close enough to see the couple standing in the middle of the
floor with the justice of the peace in front of them pronouncing the
ceremony; and we went to the dining room, where we stood around
awkwardly and watched the grown-ups eat. Finally, after most of the
food had been cleaned up, someone noticed us and gave us two liberal
pieces of pumpkin pie. When we finished, nearly everyone had left
the house, so we went over to Merrill's store, where we loafed for two
hours, looking at a box of figs on display and hoping that something
eventful would happen. We were generously repaid for our patience
when the J.P. came in and asked for his fee. Merrill asked how much
he owed, and the justice quickly replied, "Two dollars." Merrill took
from his pocket a roll of one-dollar bills, peeled off two of them and
in a casual, spendthrift manner gave them with a lavish hand to Squire
Blount. Walton and I were overcome with surprise at the amount of
the fee and the don't-care-how-much-it-cost way that Merrill handled
his money. In fact, our astonishment was so great that we had to go
outside and talk over the matter. The sum of money received was out
of all proportion to the time given and the services rendered. It had
taken the Squire less than ten minutes to tie the knot, yet he had drawn
about half a week's pay for his "work." The groom had not seemed at
all surprised at the size of the fee asked and had not raised any protest,
but had peeled off the bills with an indifference which showed his
familiarity with handling large sums of money. His behavior and the

princely way in which he rewarded Squire Blount elicited our warmest admiration and furnished us with an agreeable topic of conversation and speculation for many days.

The sound of pianos, organs, and trumpets had never been heard in the Leatherwoods. Even violins were unknown—but everybody knew the sound of a fiddle. The country fiddler was an important personage, looked upon with almost as much respect and reverence as the country parson. His vocabulary in the way of tunes was rather limited, but he played the few he knew like a house afire. "Mandy Lockett," "Ole Dan Tucker," "Ryestraw," "Arkansaw Traveler," "Old Molly Hare," "Fisher's Hornpipe," "The Devil's Dream," "Soldier's Joy," and "Turkey in the Straw" were his classics.

In the fall and winter there was an occasional dance at some home in the City Rock neighborhood, and everybody in the community who wanted to attend invited himself—it was free for all. The old-fashioned square dance was the only step our backwoods folks knew, and they threw themselves into it with fury. Fighting fire was a mild and gentle exercise compared to it.

The fiddler brought his fiddle and bow tied up in a pillow case to guard the delicate tone of the instrument against the weather. When he had tuned up the fiddle, rosined his bow, and got all set, and when the dancing broke out, some obliging young man got two knitting needles and beat a tattoo on the strings as the fiddler played—a trick that was supposed to liven up the music and to put mettle into the heels of the dancers. It was pretty! Girls with good looks and those nimble on their feet were in demand as partners and danced nearly every "set," while clumsy girls, if any, were neglected.

I recall a dance at the home of Charlie Benbrook, later in life Dr. C. E. Benbrook, in the City Rock neighborhood, that was full of interest and excitement. Major Reynolds was the fiddler, the only one within a radius of ten miles, and with him was his grown daughter Emma, who had had the misfortune, years before, of getting one of her hands cut off in a sorghum mill. She loved to dance, she always came to the dances with her father, and she was well liked; but the young men shunned her as a partner because they found it awkward or embarrassing to "swing on the corners and all promenade" with her because of her arm.

The dance had been in full swing for only an hour or so when suddenly the fiddler quit playing, put his fiddle in the pillow case and began tying it up. The young men gathered about him in vigorous protest and called his attention to the fact that it was still early in the night. They asked for an explanation and got none. In sullen silence he continued to tie up his fiddle in the pillow slip. Dow Harris quickly sensed the cause of his behavior and lost no time in trying a remedy. He walked over to the fiddler's daughter and asked her to dance with him. She promptly accepted, and they stepped out onto the floor. Then in a rather loud voice Harris begged the old man to "give us just one more tune, Major—we want to dance one more set." Mr. Reynolds looked up, and seeing his daughter, who had been neglected up to that time, standing beside Harris, he promptly untied the pillow case, took out his fiddle, tuned up the instrument, rosined his bow, bit off a chew of tobacco, and lit into some of the liveliest dance music that ever rent the unoffending air in our neighborhood.

Before the set ended, other young men held a conference outside the house and bound themselves by solemn compact that they would thereafter take turns dancing with Emma, notwithstanding difficulties, for the rest of the night. They almost danced her to exhaustion, engaging her for every set thereafter. They also worked her father hard, for he gave them fast and furious music until the early morning hours, when the young people went home happy as song birds and praising Harris for his more or less delicate diplomacy.

During the evening three young men from the north side of the White River dropped in. One of them was a stranger, set off from the crowd by his broad-brimmed hat and light boots; none of us had ever seen him before. I speak of "us," but I do not know how I came to be at the dance. At ten I was too young to dance, and besides I didn't know how. But I was there, and probably in the way. While the revelers were having a little resting-spell between the sets, giving the fiddler and his now popular daughter a recess, Dow Harris, the hero of the evening and the best dancer in our neighborhood, stepped out onto the floor and began to entertain us with a solo exhibition. He did not know very many steps, but he was fairly adept and a pleasing figure to watch. The stranger referred to must have sat and looked on for five minutes, when suddenly he fairly leaped out into the middle of the floor and began to dance beside Dow. He was a handsome young man, with glossy black curly hair and a complexion ruddy with health; he was unusually graceful, and as nimble as an acrobat. His dancing at first was restrained and easy. Harris soon took his seat, as he realized he was no longer an attraction, and like the rest of us he was entranced by the performance of this stranger, who was now warming up to his work and doing some unusual dancing. His performance was sometimes quiet, almost noiseless, his body nearly motionless, his legs and feet going like lightning; then he would suddenly break out into a veritable storm of activity, ending up in a breath-taking climax, backward and forward, here and there, this side then that, up and down, now almost still, now active in every muscle of his body, his feet all the while working in perfect rhythm and making quite a clatter against the floor; now he would execute a "double-shuffle," "cut the pigeon's wing," and finally whirl into astonishing leaps and spins the likes of which we had never seen before.

When he was about to end his exhibition Mr. Reynolds seized his fiddle and played "The Arkansaw Traveler" for him, putting every bit of fire and energy he had into it, and the dancer responded in kind. He danced the very life out of that lively and inspiring old tune and won the admiration and praise of saint and sinner alike. When he quit the floor and sat down, all of us realized we had witnessed a remarkable exhibition. I have seen a good many dancers perform on the stage and on the screen since that night, but no dancer has given me half as thrilling an experience as did the romantic young man at Benbrook's. The stranger was Rufus P. Jones, just arrived from Texas. He became a citizen of Izard County, married a daughter of the late Capt. R. C. Matthews of Pineville, and died a few years ago at his home near Calico Rock.

This was the most memorable square dance I ever attended.

It was a pleasant summer day several years later when Uncle took Ellen and Walton and me to Mountain Home for a visit in the home of Dr. Wallis. We knew that there was a piano in his home, although I have no recollection of how we learned about it. We had never seen a piano nor heard one, and we spent a good part of the day as we drove along the road speculating about the instrument and wondering if we would get to hear it. Just about dusk, after we had arrived and were out feeding our horses, some musical notes floated out on the air and caught our ears. We halted feeding operations instantly, and Walton exclaimed, "Listen, they're tunin' her up." We had seen fiddles and knew that they had to be tuned before playing and supposed that pianos had to be tuned up in the same way. To our great enjoyment we were presently invited into the parlor, and Miss Ella Wallis played several "tunes" for us.

Being greenhorns from the sticks caused us to make a good many blunders, but I don't recall that it ever caused us much embarrassment—at least we were not intimidated. A day or two after Miss Ella tuned the piano for us I saw a placard over a wooden bin in Dr. Wallis's store that read, "Peanuts 5c a pint." I was familiar with walnuts and hickorynuts and hazelnuts and chinquapins, but here was something new: I had never heard of peanuts, and my curiosity led me to invest five cents. The clerk, George Wallis, scooped out a pint and started to hand them over the counter to me when I caught sight of them. "Hold on," I said; "them's goobers; I don't want no goobers, we raise 'em by the bushel every year." I was right: we grew a crop of goober-peas every year, but never before had I heard them called peanuts. Needless to say, my ignorance brought on hearty laughs in Wallis's store.

In the following winter Walton and I were treated to a visit to Batesville. It was the largest city we had ever seen, boasting more than a thousand inhabitants. The weather was cold, but we were wearing our straw hats, bought in the summer. In front of Johnny Cannon's bakery and confection store we noticed a sign bearing the legend: "Ice Cream 10c." We had heard of ice cream and we knew it was good to eat, but we had never seen any of it and had no idea what it looked like. Was it solid or liquid? Was it served in bottles or on plates? Walton and I took counsel and decided to invest five cents each in it, but as I had no idea how to order it and did not want to blunder, I told Walton he could ask for it. He called out, "We want a glass of ice cream." Mrs. Cannon told him that ice cream was not served in the winter, and Walton saved face by hotly countering: "Then why don't you take down your sign out there?"

When I was twenty a Batesville merchant invited a friend of mine, Henry B. Jeffery, and me to spend Christmas in Batesville with him. We gladly accepted the invitation, and arrived at the town on Christmas Eve. During the next few days we had quite a famous time, highlighted by a roller-skating party. Skating was the popular pastime in Batesville, and a good rink had been fitted up on the second floor of Maxfield's store. Jeffery and I went to the rink merely to watch this novel sport, not to skate, but we quickly saw that it was so easy and fascinating that we became eager to try it and asked two of the young men who were taking a brief rest if we could borrow some skates. They agreed so readily, I might say enthusiastically, that our suspicions should have been aroused; but we were from the sticks and were entirely unsuspecting. They immediately got us each a pair of skates and very generously began giving us instructions. The best way to begin, they explained, was to sit down flat on the floor and put the skates on, as we would get a good deal of valuable practice in getting to our feet. Putting them on was easy enough, and we confidently expected to be circling the room with the other skaters in a few minutes. Our instructors were correct in telling us that we would get practice by trying to get to our feet from a sitting position, as it took us fully ten minutes to gain an erect posture for the first time, however briefly. The struggle to rise on feet that would not catch hold of the floor made us feel pretty helpless. In our efforts to stand we skinned our knees and bumped other parts of our anatomy but our friends cheered us on heartily. We tried to help each other, but our efforts worked badly, for when one would get on his feet and undertake to assist the other, his feet would fly from under him as the other was straightening up. So we seesawed back and forth for some time, one going up and the other down, and sometimes both going down together. Meanwhile our instructors, who had now increased in number, gathered around to shout encouragement to us, telling us we were doing well, were learning much faster than most skaters.

Finally, with the aid of a chair, we both got to our feet, and then the fun commenced. Our feet would spread apart sideways and we would have no end of trouble bringing them together; then one foot would turn west while the other went north, in this way getting us into awkward, not to say strenuous, situations. Once again our instructors offered their kindly suggestions. They told us that the quickest way to learn to roller-skate was to hold onto one end of a rope while at the other end a good skater pulled us along. We fell for the suggestion. The moment our instructor, one of the accommodating young men, would go forward, we would pull back on the rope, our feet would shoot out from under us, and the floor would fly up and hit us in the middle of the back a fraction of a second later. After a few severe jolts our enthusiasm for learning to skate began to cool. Sensing this, the young men advised us that we were making a mistake in pulling back on the rope—we ought to lean forward. Thus encouraged, we tried again, this time leaning forward as our leader started off. When he gave a little tug now and then, we left our feet behind and pitched forward on our already bruised and aching knees.

At length we saw two of the skaters laughing as they turned the curve of the rink. So we held a conference and decided that our instructors were planning to put something over on us, something that would make us look ridiculous, and that we wouldn't stand for it. We would take off our skates and thwart their plan. We would show them that even if we were from the tall timber, they couldn't make fools of us.

Some years after I left the Leatherwoods, I attended a session of the Circuit Court in Stone County at which a young man was on trial for disturbing public worship in the Baptist Church at Red Stripe. Attending the trial with me was an old friend, Dennis Dozier, and the trial lawyers were friends of many years: Judge Fulkerson was in the Chair, Emmet Jeffrey was Prosecuting Attorney, and B. F. Williamson was Defense Counsel. The key witness for the prosecution was an old lady who testified that before entering the church she had seen the defendant acting giddily, had watched him enter the church and take a seat near the door, where he smirked and talked to the boys on either side of him while the services were going on. Later she had seen him get up and walk unsteadily down the aisle, stagger, in fact, to about the center of the house, where he again seated himself and laughed and talked to those around him. She had been considerably disturbed by his conduct. Asked if others had been disturbed, she said she couldn't speak for them, but they appeared to be greatly disturbed.

The defense attorney then undertook to destroy her testimony with a well-contrived plan of attack that seemed likely to succeed.

"Where was the defendant when you first saw him?"

"I first seen him outside in front of the church."

"What was he doing?"

"Cuttin' up like a fool."

"And you saw him come inside?"

"I did."

"How could you see him come inside if you were facing the preacher?"

"I was settin' on a bench at the left facin' the pulpit and I seen him come in."

"Did you watch to see what he did after he came inside?"

"Yes, I watched him."

"What did you see?"

"He come staggerin' in an' when he sot down he said somethin' to the boys he was settin' by. I don't know what he said, but they sniggered out loud at him."

"What did he do next?"

"He got up an' come down about half-way the house an' sot down agin.' He was staggerin' as he come and he like to fell in old Miss Spencer's lap."

"What did he do after he sat down?"

"He grinned an' whispered half out loud and kep' it up when the preacher was exhortin' and even durin' the prayer."

"Was anybody disturbed by his conduct?"

"Well, he disturbed me a heap. I couldn't listen at what the preacher was sayin' fer watchin' him an' his foolishness."

"Your Honor, it is only human nature for us to see in others what we are looking for. If we look for faults we can usually find them, and if we look for good points we can find them just as easily. The witness who has just testified is a good woman, a splendid woman, and she would never deliberately misrepresent what she saw. But she appears to be the only one who was upset by the defendant's behavior—she happened to see him outside the church "cuttin' up," she said, "like a fool." It's perfectly natural for young men his age to cut up now and then and there's nothing wrong with cutting up outside a church. Yet the language the good woman used showed that she was very much displeased with his innocent, boyish behavior, and she got it in for him then and there. And so she watched him, according to her own testimony, she watched him come into the church, she watched him sit down, watched him while the services were going on, watched him from start to finish, looking for something bad, looking for faults in his behavior.

"Now why was this good woman not listening to the preacher instead of watching this young man?" Why did she not spend this hour in worship? Even during the prayer she was watching, looking for something to criticize. If she had been singing and praying and listening to the preacher, she would not have been disturbed that day."

This sharp line of cross-questioning had placed the star witness for the prosecution in unfavorable light, and everyone in the courtroom sensed it.

Prosecuting Attorney Jeffery's rejoinder was brief. "The Defense Counsel," he said, "has not dared to question a single statement that this good woman has made. Instead he has tried to break down her testimony by telling you and this jury of sensible, God-fearing men that she did too much watching and that she should have been praying instead of watching. When did it become a crime for Christian people to watch? We can't be too watchful in seeing to it that the worship of God is given full respect. Ah, gentlemen of the jury, that Good Book that we all love, that is dearer to us than life itself, says to you and to me and to all of us: '*Watch and pray*.' That's the word of God, gentlemen: 'WATCH as well as pray.' "

I turned at once to my friend Dozier and whispered to him: "Jeffery's got him—he's guilty; it's all over." And it was.

The jury took about five minutes to deliberate and the verdict was announced: "We find the defendant guilty."

Chapter X
Steamboating on the Upper White in 1886

I could have been content to live forever on the farm, but not as a plowhand or cotton-chopper. I liked the trees, vines, and flowers, the animals both wild and domestic, the springs, the creeks; but making a crop did not have much appeal to me. Since Walton liked farming no better than I did, all of us understood that when he and I reached the age of twenty-one we would leave the Swans' home and find places for ourselves in the life beyond the Leatherwoods, about which we knew so little. What was I to do? Where was I to go? Steamboating had its attractions for me but it seemed beyond reach. Very early I decided upon an occupation and confided my ambitions to Walton. I hoped to rise to the dizzy heights of clerk in a candy store. My plans were received with derision by Walton, who doubted that I could ever reach such an exalted position. Occasionally when we were out in the cotton field lazily hoeing a row of cotton a quarter of a mile long, I would say, "Well, six years from today I won't be here workin' in the hot sun. I'll be behind the counter."

"Yes, you'll be on the farm pullin' the lines over old Beck."

"And where will you be?"

"I'll be bossin' you and the other hands."

At the age of seventeen I got a job teaching the three-month school which was located a quarter of a mile from our home. Unlike the subscription schools that I had attended, this was the new-type "free" school. My salary was $25 a month, a handsome sum for that day and much more than I was worth. With lingering shame I realize and acknowledge that I was a very poor teacher. The first day of the term I made a concession to the dignity of the calling by wearing shoes, but that was the only time I wore them. Young women eighteen years old who attended my school came barefooted, so I bowed to social convention and did likewise the rest of the term. Dudes would not have been looked upon with favor in our community.

At the end of the session I had done only one deed that I could look back upon with satisfaction—the licking I gave Walton, who was my pupil and who therefore could not defend himself against my switch. Though we were "brothers," and though I had no specific scores to even against him, the opportunity was too tempting. So when a legitimate occasion arose, I took advantage of it. I did not cause him much physical discomfort, but I did assert my superiority and for many days looked back with pleasure upon a good performance.

Then when I was nineteen I got a job working in Aiken's store at Calico Rock for $6.25 a month plus board—which was quite as much as I was worth, though I did not think so. It was one p.m. on a Saturday when I started work, and at five I asked to get off until Monday morning. From Saturday until Monday I debated whether to go back to my job at Aiken's or to stay home and plant corn. I decided to farm. On the following Thursday when I was out in the field planting corn Mr. Aiken rode up, dismounted, and walked toward me. I braced myself for the rebuke I deserved and felt sure he was going to give me for quitting my job at his store without giving him notice. He was wearing his Sunday clothes. I was in rough homespuns, barefooted, with pants rolled up. He walked briskly to me, extended his hand in cordial greeting, expressed regret that I had decided not to work for him, and said that perhaps at some other time we could come to agreeable terms. When winter came I was back behind the counter at Aiken's store. After I had worked there for a few months he suggested that I go to St. Louis and take a book-keeping and banking course in Bryant and Stratton's Business College. Uncle approved, and I sent for the prospectus, which looked good to me. I totaled up my resources and found that I lacked about $125 of having enough money to cover my expenses for the three-and-a-half-month session. As Uncle had sent Ellen and me to the Mountain Home Academy, he was not able to give much help. One day it occurred to me that I might get the money from Captain R. C. Matthews, a retired merchant of Pineville and an old friend of my parents. So I borrowed a horse from Mr. Aiken and went to see the Captain. Though twenty years of age, I was very green at dealing with my elders and not at all sure of myself. I found him at home and told him my prospects and plans. I think he suspected that I had come to ask for a loan, and he wanted me to make the application without any encouragement from him. He said that my plans looked sound to him and then asked, "Why don't you go and take this business course?"

I had not mentioned finances and was hoping he would ask if I needed money. I was now in a corner and had to face the issue. So I said, "It will take more money than I've got, Captain Matthews."

He replied, "How do you expect to go then, if you haven't got enough money?"

That question, asked in a cold, blunt manner, staggered me, but I answered, "I thought I'd see if I could borrow $125 from you for six months."

The Captain looked at me sternly and asked, "What kind of security can you give me?"

I had not thought of that important matter. I had no security to offer him, and said, "I will give you my note, drawing ten per cent interest and I will pay you back in six months."

Captain Matthews looked me straight in the eye for half a minute and said, "Well, I'll take a chance on you." He pulled out a drawer, got a blank note, filled it out, and gave it to me to sign. After I put my name on it, he went to a small safe, took out a box, counted out $125 in bills and handed them to me (checks were not used in the Leatherwoods). I thanked him and hurried away, prouder than I had ever been in my life.

That was in the latter part of August. In early September I enrolled in the St. Louis business college and graduated in December 1885 as I was celebrating my twenty-first birthday. A few days before my graduation, President W. M. Carpenter called me into his office and offered me the management of the business college in St. Charles, Missouri. Though I felt competent to handle the job, I was homesick. I wanted to see the blue hills and blue streams of north Arkansas so much that had I been offered the job as head office manager for Standard Oil I would have declined. So back to my native hills I went and within a month found a job as clerk on the Steamer *Home*, which plied the waters of the upper White River. I could not have been more happy.

To me there is nothing more picturesque than a handsome steamboat coming into port, her exhaust pipes alternately puffing billows of white vapor, her two large smokestacks pouring forth great volumes of black smoke, the Stars and Stripes floating gently from the flagstaff, the hurricane deck lined with passengers exchanging noisy greetings with friends on shore, the master standing by the big bell on the forward pilot deck giving orders and signals to the pilot and mate, the bells jangling in the engine room, and the great paddlewheel kicking up white sprays of water as it pushes the boat toward the landing. In full career she is just as handsome, during either daylight hours or at night when her many lights shine through the darkness.

In the 1870s, '80s, and '90s none of the packets built for the upper White River were imposing in size, but many large and commodious boats, the so-called "floating palaces," most of them from Memphis, St. Louis, Cincinnati, and New Orleans, dashed in during high water for trips as far up as Buffalo City. Including the pilot houses the larger boats were four stories high. First there was the main deck, which carried most of the freight and the deck passengers. Above this was the boiler deck where the cabins or staterooms for the passengers, the dining room, bar, offices, cook's pantry, and storage rooms were located. Next was the hurricane deck on which was the texas, consisting of the cabins and staterooms of the officers of the boat. Atop the texas was the pilot house, that gave the pilot an unobstructed view fore and aft and on the sides. Forever linked in memory with the boats are the famous whistles, located above the roofs on the pilot houses. They usually had three prongs, each prong keyed to a different pitch, and were very musical. If atmospheric conditions were favorable, they could be heard for a distance of twenty-five miles. The *Josie Harry* had a five-prong whistle that had been heard, so I was told, for fifty miles. The cost of the big boats ran up to about $100,000. The masters of some of the more luxurious steamers boasted to me about the cost of the furnishings of the dining rooms and staterooms. For example, I was told of velvets for the cabins costing eleven dollars a yard, a price almost beyond belief in those days.

Travel by steamboat anywhere was doubtless a romantic experience. There was a charm about it that one does not feel on a train or in an automobile. When one boarded a boat, he knew that he was to have a leisurely trip and was prepared to enjoy the beauty of the scenery and the society of new acquaintances. To stand out on the white clean deck by the side of the master or by the big bell, or to lean against a spar, or to clutch a guy-rope as the boat pushed steadily forward or swung slowly into port and to exchange greetings with strangers or friends on shore gave one a deep pleasure and a deep satisfaction that time does not erase.

On the upper White River, traveling by steamboat offered additional attractions. I wonder if this was not steamboating at its best. The River is navigable for five hundred miles, and its upper half winds through the beautiful Ozark Mountains. For one with any love of beauty in his make-up a trip on the upper White, the clearest of all the rivers in Mid-America, was an unforgettable experience. Here a stately mountain sloped back from the water's edge to its blue summit hundreds of feet above; there a great bluff of gray granite towered or leaned over the River; yonder a wide bend in the River brought into view a valley with blue mountains beyond it. In the spring the hills were alive with the bloom of redbud, dogwood, wild plum, mountain ash, and wild azalea; in the summer the varied greens of a hundred kinds of trees, where axe had never fallen, covered the hills, and late on summer evenings the blue of distant hills turned to lavender; in the fall the mountains put on their finest show of all, with many shades of red and gold intermingled; and in the winter dark cedars and pines stood out against the grays and browns of the hill-sides. But the main feature of every scene was the River, blue-clear, forever winding among the hills.

Before the advent of the steamboats, commerce with the outside world had been very difficult. The case of Asa McFelich will serve to illustrate. A Scot born in Ohio, he came to the Ozarks about 1826 and settled at the mouth of Swan Creek, now the site of Forsythe, Missouri. During the falls and early winters he bought up all available produce along the River, such as hides, furs, dried venison, buffalo and bear meat, bear oil, and wild honey and floated it by keel-boat to New Orleans, where he found a ready market. After disposing of his produce he bought stocks of goods to trade to the Indians, trappers, hunters, and the handful of pioneers who had made their homes along the White, and poled his keel-boat with its cargo back up the Mississippi to the White and up the White to his home. The keel-boats, which ranged from one to thirty tonners, were usually propelled by one, two, or three men on each side, who set long poles against the bottom of the River while holding the other end of the poles against their shoulders. In this position they would walk from bow to stern, pushing against their poles. After steamboats began navigating the Mississippi, he would have his keel-boat towed up the River to the mouth of the White and would pole it the rest of the way, a maximum distance of five hundred and twenty miles. Perhaps there are Americans today hardy enough to undertake an annual trip like this one to New Orleans. The round trip required six months.

During the last third of the nineteenth century steamboating was a highly developed business on the upper White. Railroads had taken over most of the traffic along the lower River, but the boats were the life-line of the Ozark country, as there was no other mode of travel or traffic in all north Arkansas except by dirt trails, which at some seasons of the year were well-nigh impassable. It was out of the question to bring in supplies by wagon. For example, it would require at least two weeks to haul ten barrels of salt round trip from Little Rock to Calico Rock, whereas a large boat out of Memphis could carry a thousand barrels of salt—enough to supply the entire section for a year—at a fraction of a cent a pound. Time required for the trip: four or five days. With the population of the Ozarks rapidly increasing during the last thirty years of the century, keelboats disappeared and steamboats on the River became numerous.

To the folks living along the White in the early days, the coming of a steamboat was a notable event. Warned of her approach by her musical whistle while she was miles away, people flocked to the River towns and other landing places well in advance of her arrival. As most of the people living along the upper River had never been more than thirty miles from their birthplaces and knew only vaguely of the luxuries of city life, their one glimpse of the world of wealth—New Orleans, Memphis, St. Louis, Cincinnati—came when the big boats steamed up the River, and especially when they tied up at the landings. Farmers often brought their whole families to Calico Rock to see and board one of the larger boats. They were permitted to go all over her and look at her mysterious equipment—the great wheel, the machinery that turned it, the boilers that generated the steam, the several decks, the lordly dining room, the pilot house, the whistle, the big bell. They could also see the distinguished officers of the boat—the captain, the master, the pilot, the mate, as well as the engineer in his greasy clothes, the fireman loading the furnace with pine, the deck-hands unloading the freight or loading the cotton.

I was three years old when I saw my first steamboat, the *Malta*. I remember calling it a wagon in the river. The following year I boarded my first steamboat—so young that I have little recollection of the incident. It was 1869 when my father took his family to see this boat, the *Argus*, which had tied up at the Calico Rock landing. I escaped from my parents and a few minutes later was found in the engine room asking to see some pineapples. I was familiar with pine trees and had heard that steamboats sold pineapples, which I supposed grew on pines. My question was prompted, it seems, when I was shown the stacks of pine firewood in the engine room.

Captain Will C. Shipp, who was looked upon as the father of White River pilots, told me that when he was eighteen (about 1848), he went to North Fork to enter school. Looking for a place to room and board, he was told to see Major Jake Wolf*, who owned a two-story cabin made of hewn pine logs, the largest house in that area. "Yes, young man, you can stay here," said Major Wolf, "if you're willin' to pay the price, but it ain't cheap. I can't get by no more on what I been a gittin'. Coffee and sugar and everything has went up in price, and the cost of livin' is so high these days that I won't even talk about askin' you less than three dollars a month for bed and board." This was driving a hard bargain, but young Shipp felt that under the circumstances he had best close the deal, and did so.

Captain Shipp knew our family well, and to please the children he always sounded the whistle of his boat exactly opposite our home in the River bottoms. When he was heading upstream this signal served as the whistle for the Calico Rock landing, one mile away. His example was followed by other pilots, and in time all the pilots who were headed up the River sounded their whistles for the landing at the same place, very much to the delight and pride of us children. During my later childhood, when steamboating was in its heyday, every boy on the upper River looked forward eagerly to the day when he would come into the port of Calico Rock standing at the wheel as pilot or on the hurricane deck as master of some fine steamboat. My own ambitions were not completely realized, but I was more than pleased to be the clerk on the steamer *Home* during the season of 1886—my first important job. The *Home* was owned and piloted by Captain T. B. Stallings, and the season I worked for him stands out in my memory as clearly as any other year of my life. Our regular run was from Batesville to Buffalo City, a distance of ninety miles, but we often went much farther up the River. The average speed of the *Home* was determined by the stage of the River—four to five miles upstream and between ten and fifteen downstream.

I began my work with great pride: my cup was full. It was all but beyond belief that at twenty-one I was an officer on a steamboat—a dream of my childhood fulfilled—on a boat plying my own White River, past the cabin on the farm in the bottoms where I was born, past the great Calico Rock, past my own Leatherwood hills, and through the scenic Ozark Mountains. Every run that we made on the River brought new discoveries without number.

*Major Wolf was the author's great-great uncle. His cabin, the oldest two-story house in Arkansas, has been restored and is open to the public in Norfork.

The duties of a clerk, I found, were not very heavy. I had to work hard on my "manifest," or list of freight, before the *Home* made her first stop after loading; and I must be up at any hour of the night for whenever and wherever the boat made a landing. I must go ashore and check off all the items that were unloaded and list the freight taken on board. Then after the boat left the landing I again had to work on my manifest, rechecking all freight just loaded or unloaded. At the landings the mate and the clerk were the two busiest officers of the boat. The mate had charge of the deck-hands who unloaded and loaded the cargo. The work had to be done quickly because expenses went on when the boat was in port except that less fuel was required. The mate therefore became a dynamo of activity, rushing out on the forecastle, furiously blustering and cursing and storming at the deck-hands, calling them a variety of picturesque and uncomplimentary names, chiefly for the benefit of the natives strung along the bank of the River. The hands understood that he was showing off, engaging in stageplay, and bore him no resentment. A half-hour later he might be found telling them jokes and playing Seven-Up with them.

Everything about steamboats and steamboating fascinated me: the musical whistle, the system of bell signals between master and engineer, the work and play of the Negroes who hauled the cargo, the skills of the pilot, and the stories of the captain, master, and pilot. Lingering in my memory are the refreshing odors on the boats. I liked the smell of a steamboat—it is a smelly place. The dining room with its rich furnishings and excellent food contributed its full share of stimulating and hunger-exciting odors. In front of the dining room were the office on one side of the hall and the bar on the other. Stocks of candy and fruit—apples, oranges, lemons, pineapples, raisins, and figs were on sale in the office, while on the other side of the hall the preparation of egg-nog, mint juleps, rock and rye, cocktails, sour toddies, and other mixed and fancy drinks calling for the use of sugar, rock candy, lemons, whiskey, water (not very much), nutmegs, and other spices produced a sweet, pungent odor that kept the olfactory nerves in a pleasant and agreeable state. I like the smell of a steamboat.

From early days the Negro played an important role in steamboat life, and without him a picturesque part would have been missing. He loved the river and the life on the steamboats. On the average there were about fifteen Negroes on the boats in the upper River trade. These included deck-hands, firemen, cooks, and cabin boys.

They were a happy, carefree lot and except when the boats were receiving or discharging freight, they led an easy life. During the day, when the boats were running, they spent a good deal of time playing Seven-Up down on the boiler deck. I loved to watch them play this old game. They would rather save a jack or catch their opponents' jack than to make high, low, and game. Each one seemed able to tell, somehow, whether his opponents held the jack, and strangely enough each had an uncanny way of knowing whether his opponents could catch his own jack. Time and again, watching a four-handed game of Seven-Up, two on a side, I have seen Joe Woods, a fat Negro who perspired freely, paste the jack, face out, on his sweaty forehead, taunting his opponents, who he knew were not able to catch it. Often at night several of the boys would shoot craps in the engine room. Arch Humphreys, a strongly built Negro, was the most successful man with the dice. Most of the hands would take a drink, but Humphreys was the only one who ever got unsteady on his feet.

The deck-hands entered heartily into the spirit of rivalry that existed among the boats and were always loyal to the boat they were on, no matter whether it was a battered has-been or a floating palace. They would pay the most handsome compliments to their own vessel—its incredible performances, its generous patronage by the merchants along the River, the lavish banquets served the crew three times a day—while making the most derogatory remarks about the other boat. I can recall enough of these taunts to put together a typical exchange. If the *John F. Allen* and the *Home* happened to meet at Calico Rock the deck-hands would compliment one another in this manner:

"Hullo, you black ape, how fuh up de ribbuh is you all been?" asks a deck-hand of the *Home*.

"We's been up to Fo'sythe, Missouri," replies the prevaricator on the *Allen*.

"You lyin'; you couln' get obah de Rap-peeds wid dat ole tub."

"When you all leave Batesville?"

"We lef dis mawnin' aftuh breakfas'."

"You lyin' yo-seff. You mean you lef' day befo' yestiddy befo' breakfas'. Dat ole wheezin', coughin' ferryboat couldn' git up heah in two days an' nights. When we gits to Batesville dis aftuhnoon I'll tell yo' folks you be back duh las' of nex' week efen you doan stahve to death befo' den."

"You means if I doan git choked to death on strawbehs an' cream."

And so the contest would run until one of the boats left port. Boats passing in midstream drew a few taunts of the same kind. In one of these colloquies between Mitch Hawkins and Abe Harris when Mitch was boasting about how many times his boat had been to Forsythe, Missouri, a passenger asked Mitch how far up the White he had been. Mitch replied, "Ise been clean up to de mouf."

The deck-hands were highly dexterous at handling freight, especially cotton. They used short cotton-hooks to pull the bales this way and that and to prevent them from rolling down from the top of the bank to the stage plank or gunwales. When the banks were steep and smooth, the hands often rode the bales down. I have seen Jim Davis (called Jim Fewclothes on the boat) ride many a bale down a slippery bank. At the top of the bank he would jump on a bale lying on its flat side and reach forward to fasten his hook in the far edge and then pull back. The boys would give the bale a shove, and down the bank and away it would go with him aboard, clear to the River, without ever a mishap.

The Negroes provided a great deal of musical entertainment. It was good to hear them break out in song at any time, but a real treat to listen to them grouped together on the boiler deck on warm nights in spring and summer, as they sang their own songs in their own way. Passengers used to gather on the decks and in doorways to listen and applaud. The singing was generally soft and slow.

I marveled at the Negroes' ability to sleep, regardless of physical disadvantages. I have seen a Negro fireman on the *Home*, when off duty on a hot summer day, crawl up on a scaffold just above the boiler, which carried a hundred and seventy-five pounds of steam, and take a long, refreshing nap.

In recent years I have asked some of the old deck-hands whether they would like to return to life on the River. The answers have been unanimously and emphatically in the affirmative. All the men I talked with are still steamboat enthusiasts and feel that when the last boat was driven from the River in 1905 they were victims of a lost cause. One of them said that if a barge line was revived on the Mississippi he was going to say goodbye to Arkansas and go straight to Memphis.

Steamboating was a rather hazardous business back in the last half of the nineteenth century, as the number of boats sunk or destroyed by fire clearly shows. The hazards were of several kinds. A good many boats burned. Many struck snags and sank. In high water there was always the danger that a log would jam the stern wheel or rudder and so render the boat helpless. Sometimes the engines failed—boilers were known to burst. But the most frequent source of trouble was the pilot, who might be inefficient, or careless, or drunk.

The pilot was the most important officer on the boat. When he was at the wheel he was supreme—not even the captain of the vessel could give him orders about the navigation of the boat. When the pilot said, "Tie up," at night or in foggy weather, the captain had to acquiesce. To know how to steer a boat was the smallest part of the pilot's qualifications—knowledge of the river was much more important. He had to know every shoal and reef, every submerged boulder and snag, every turn in the main channel, every bend and tow-head* and point. He must be familiar with high- and low-water currents and must know how close to shore he could safely steer his boat. If he was going upstream he must avoid the swift currents where progress was slow and constantly shift his position, crossing from side to side to take advantage of the slower water near the banks and under the lee of islands and promontories. He must also know how his boat would respond under varying conditions of the river.

Perhaps the reason that so few boats on the upper White came to grief was that the pilots were an unusually skillful company. I became personally acquainted with about twenty of them, including a number of the most experienced. Captain Will Shipp was always spoken of with the highest regard—almost reverence—as the "father" of pilots, the faultless pilot, the master teacher, unsurpassed in skill at handling a boat. He began his career on the River by piloting keelboats, and for the rest of his life he followed the steamboat trade on the upper White, from its beginnings in the late 1840s or early '50s to its demise in 1905, when the Iron Mountain Railroad paralleling the River was opened. It was facetiously said of him as illustrating his knowledge of the River that if someone should break a branch off a tree and show it to him, he could tell what tree it was from and where the tree was located. He was known in all the River towns from Forsythe, Missouri, to the mouth of the White and was quite at home on the Mississippi from St. Louis to New Orleans. Old rivermen loved to tell tales of his remarkable feats of piloting. Captain E. B. Warner was another pilot credited with fabulous performances. When he was a young man, he was considered the most brilliant and daring pilot on the River. He had such confidence in himself that he would take chances

---

*A tow-head is a sandbar thickly covered with cottonwoods or willows.

on dark nights and on dangerous stretches of the River that no other pilot would consider. Captain Stallings told me that he was aboard when Captain Warner steered his boat down through the Buffalo Shoals, known for its swift and tortuous channel, shallow waters, and dangerous boulders, on a black night, yet not once did the boat scrape the bottom or touch a boulder. Captain Will Warner piloted the *John F. Allen* for two years and never put a scratch or scar on her—a remarkable record. Captain Stallings took his boat, the *Lady Boone*, four miles up the Buffalo River and brought her out safely. This was the first attempt to navigate that wild and dangerous mountain stream, so full of boulders and rapids. But Captain Will Warner e-clipsed that record by steering his boat, the *Dauntless*, up the Buffalo twelve miles, carrying a shipment of machinery for a zinc-mining company near the mouth of Rush Creek. This record is certain to stand for all time.

For White River pilots the shoals were the chief problem and the chief danger. On one of my first trips up the River I was introduced to a very ingenious maneuver of the pilot in doing the impossible. It seems incredible that a boat drawing, let us say, three feet of water can be literally "jumped" over a shoal where the water is only two and a half feet deep, but I have seen it done several times. The first time was at the Wolf Bayou Shoal, sixteen miles above Batesville, where the heavily loaded *Home* ran aground. Captain Stallings ordered the mate to lay a line to a tree some three hundred and fifty feet up the River. With the other end of the cable around the capstan, the steam was turned on and the cable was wound around the capstan until it was taut—almost to the breaking point. In the meantime the pilot had slow-belled the engine, so that the big stern wheel was turning forward very slowly, keeping the water pulled from under the boat as she lay hard on the bottom. Then the pilot rang the stopping bell and immediately rang the backing bell. The engineer reversed the wheel and quickly backed with all his power. The result of these maneuvers was that the backing of the wheel forced a great volume of water under the boat, lifting her clear of the River bottom, so that the tautness of the cable literally jerked her forward several feet. The slack in the cable was quickly taken up to hold what had been gained, and the maneuver was repeated until the reef was cleared.

As the upper White is a mountain river, there are swift, shallow shoals every few miles. Most of these shoals bear picturesque names, suggested by appearance, local conditions, or local traditions. The principal ones were Hungry John, Fattybread, Haggletooth, Cackling Pullet, Blue Streak, Buck Island, Sam's Shoal, The Rap-peeds (Rapids), Calico Rock, Buffalo, and Bull Creek. Other "bad places" in the River were Nellie's Apron, Dark Corners, Lost Hollow, Fish Trap, Devil's Tea Table, and Tar Trough.

Although the regular run of the *Home* was from Batesville to Buffalo City, we often went far above Buffalo, and the farther we went the more difficult and dangerous became the navigation. The Bull Creek Shoals, about thirty miles above Buffalo City, were the most difficult that the Steamer *Home* encountered while I was clerk. The level of the River dropped some fifteen feet within a mile. There was ample water in the channel, but the current was so swift that the *Home* could not move upstream. She had climbed over the Buffalo Shoals the evening before with six hundred barrels of salt on board without laying a line. We had put off four hundred barrels of the salt at McBee's Landing, and now with but two hundred barrels aboard she was stalled at Bull Creek. A line was laid and still she could not go over. We were allowed to carry only one hundred and seventy-five pounds of steam in her boilers, but the engineer, a daredevil fellow, ran the steam up to two hundred and twenty-five pounds by wedging a block of wood in between the safety-valve "pop-off" and the deck above, thus rendering the safety-valve useless. The boilers became so hot that he had to keep the "doctor" or pump running the whole time we were going over to keep the boilers supplied with water. But over we went through the swift water. The situation was so dangerous that when the boat chanced to come close to the shore I put out a plank and jumped off to terra firma.

The closest escape we had while I was on the *Home* occurred when I was in the pilot house talking with Captain Stallings, who was at the wheel. We had just succeeded in climbing the Buffalo Shoals by "jumping" the boat over the last ledge at the head of the shoals and were getting into deeper water, about four feet but still very swift, when the Captain heard a sudden noise in the engine room. Immediately the stern wheel stopped. I did not know what had happened, but the Captain did. "Here, take this wheel," he said excitedly, "and keep her headed straight up the River." He bounded out of the pilot house and down the stairs to the hurricane deck, where there was a large coil of cable that had not been used. He heaved it over the banister to the boiler deck below and ran down the stairs. By the time he reached the prow of the boat the deck hands were tying the cable onto the anchor, making ready to heave it over. Although no commands had been given, they had sensed the danger and acted immediately. They dragged the anchor quickly to the edge and heaved it overboard. The river bed here and all along its mile of shoal water is a mass of boulders. Before the boat had drifted forty seconds the anchor caught a large boulder and held fast. We had already been swept back into the swift current, and had the anchor not held, the *Home* would have been wrecked within five minutes in that crooked, narrow channel. What had happened to the machinery was that, in steamboat parlance, the valve had "slipped," and the engineer could not turn on the steam. Consequently the stern wheel had gone dead.

Like the other White River packets the *Home* used cordwood, principally pine, for fuel. Enterprising farmers hauled it from the woods and stacked it in cords on the river banks during the later summer and fall when few boats were running, or in case of drouth no boats at all, and when there was little farm work to do. A cord of wood (8' x 4' x 4') sold for four dollars. Pine knots, which ignite quickly and give a hot fire, made up a large part of every cord. When the fireman saw that his stock of fuel was running low, he would warn the mate, who would keep lookout for cordwood along the bank and signal the pilot to push in to shore at the first wood-yard he sighted. The owner of the wood was usually not present, though the whistle of the boat sometimes brought him to the landing. But no matter—he would present himself and his bill at some convenient landing on the next trip of the boat. Strangely enough, such a thing as stealing wood corded up on the river bank was unknown. It sometimes happened on account of accidents or other delays that the fuel on the boat became exhausted with no wood-yard in sight. Under such circumstances the boat would land alongside a farm (there was usually a farm on one side of the River and always a mountain or bluff on the other) and take on board as many panels of the farmer's rail fence as he needed—at a good price. I recall that once, far in the night, a boat landed at the lower end of our farm and took one thousand cedar rails. When a boat stopped for fuel the deck-hands would fly into the wood and fling it down the river bank, then carry it aboard and stack it close around the furnace for the convenience of the fireman.

Sam Ivy, who had been a schoolmate of mine at Spring Creek, thought to turn a few honest dollars one autumn by cutting and hauling cordwood for the boats. As the River was rather low for boating, he stacked his pine on the bank at the Calico Rock landing until he had built up several cords, after hauling it about three miles with a yoke of oxen. When he brought in a load, he would sit down beside it and look vainly down the River for a steamboat. One day late in the fall I was with Sam as he brought in a load of pine, corded it up, and sat down at the end of it to watch for a boat. In my early enthusiasm for steamboats, I had learned to give a good imitation of the whistle. Seeing the disconsolate Sam sitting by his cordwood, watching, waiting, and yearning for the coming of a boat so that he could cash in on his labors, I decided to give him a little temporary encouragement. I slipped around to the far end of the wood and softly emitted the three blasts of a steamboat signaling a landing. Sam exclaimed, ''There she comes,'' and jumped up, certain that the boat was near. He hurried to his wagon, cracked his whip over the heads of his lazy oxen, yelled, ''git up,'' and away he went for another load of pine knots. When he returned late in the afternoon and found no boat at the landing, he was so sorely puzzled and chagrinned that I did not have the courage to tell him that I had perpetrated the trick on him. Besides, he was bigger and stronger than I was. Sam did not have to wait many weeks before he sold his cordwood.

One of the pleasures of steamboating was sitting in the pilot house or on a deck during periods of leisure and listening to experienced pilots and captains tell amusing, exciting, and tragic stories of life on the River. Every boat—and well over a hundred plied the waters of the White—had an interesting history, and Captain Stallings would sometimes talk for hours about the adventures of the boats and the crews that manned them. One night he told of an unusual mishap which befell a Mississippi boat that made the mistake of venturing up the White. In the spring of 1874 *The Trader*, a Memphis stern-wheeler, came up the White River with freight for Buffalo City and a good list of passengers. It was an ideal time to make such a trip, for the hillsides were colored with blooming trees. The River at Batesville showed a good boating stage, but by the time *The Trader* reached North Fork the water was getting rather thin. After passing over the North Fork Shoal, one of the shallowest on the River, and going on to Shipp's Ferry, six miles above, the Captain decided to turn back and tie up at North Fork. But it was dark before *The Trader* reached the landing, and the pilot thought it unsafe to take his boat through the shoal in the dark. He therefore gave orders to tie up until the next morning and eased his boat over to the long gravel bar on the right bank of the River and went to bed.

Unfortunately he did not know the ways of mountain rivers, which rise and fall very quickly. At five o'clock the following morning the boat was resting on the gravel bar thirty feet from the water. And this was not the worst of it, for the long drouth of 1874 set in, and the helpless *Trader* sat on the treeless gravel waste for thirteen long months before there was sufficient rise in the River to float her out. The passengers and some of the officers and crew went to Batesville in yawls while the others stayed with *The Trader*, putting in their ample time painting, repairing, and caulking the boat. No pilot making regular runs on the Upper White, said Captain Stallings, would have got his boat into such a predicament.

Another story that he told was about how Captain Albert Cravens saved his life with a dive. Captain Cravens was once coming down the River above Buffalo City in a canoe with two companions when the River was almost out of banks. The three men considered themselves fortunate when they saw the *Lady Boone*—Captain Stallings, master—coming upstream. They signaled the pilot that they wished to be taken on board, and the pilot promptly responded with three short blasts of the whistle. The mate gave the deck hands hurried instructions to stand by and seize the men in the canoe as soon as they came within reach. The current was very swift, and the canoe was rapidly bearing down on the steamboat. The *Lady Boone* had a square bow, which made it difficult and dangerous to take passengers off a canoe in midstream with the River at flood stage. Captain Cravens was seated in the stern of the canoe, steering. His two companions were crouching in the bow, ready to leap aboard the steamer with the assistance of the deck-hands. When the canoe was within three feet of the steamboat they reached out and were seized by the deck-hands and pulled safely aboard. At the same instant the bow of the canoe was pushed under the bow of the *Boone*, and the stern thrust high in the air. Captain Cravens was catapulted into the River at about the center of the steamer's bow. He was instantly sucked under the boat and felt himself bumping up against the bottom as the swift current rushed him along on his ninety-five-foot submarine journey. In a moment he heard the paddles of the wheel at the stern of the boat and knew he would be killed by them unless he contrived to get clear of the wheel. Quickly he dived down, it seemed to him fifty feet down, as he afterwards said. Then he heard the wheel pass over him and knew that he was clear of the boat. By this time he was desperate for air, and he swam strongly to the surface, coming up right in the midst of the big waves that follow in the wake of a steamboat. Immediately he swam for the shore and clung to the overhanging branch of a willow tree until he was rescued by two men in a yawl from the *Boone*. "By using his head," said Captain Stallings, "he saved it."

Every boat owner had his loyal friends along the River who favored him and his boat with their patronage. As a rule, however, shippers were so eager to get their goods in and their cotton out that they were willing for the first boat that called to handle their freight. Unless we had a rainy summer, boating season opened in the winter months. At the close of the season in late summer the boats would tie up in some River town or go into the trade on some other river. The merchants on the upper White went to market once a year to buy their year's supply of "seasonable" goods, which the boats usually brought in around the first of January. The cotton-ginning season began in October and continued for two or three months. By the time the late fall or early winter rains had brought the River to a good boating stage, the entire cotton crop would have been ginned and put on the River bank for shipment. The first boat to make the run upstream would get all the cotton it could carry at the first few landings and usually enjoyed the additional advantage of getting the unconsigned freight that had accumulated at Batesville, where the railroad line from the south ended.

In the winter of 1885-86 the River was frozen over, a most unusual occurrence, and three steamboats, the *Alberta No. 3*, the *John F. Allen*, and the *Home* were lying at the wharf at Batesville, waiting for a thaw. Much freight consigned to the upper River had accumulated there, and much cotton was lying on the banks upstream awaiting shipment. The three boats had everything in readiness for a quick get-away. Presently the weather moderated, a warm rain set in, and the ice began to break up. Late in the afternoon Captain Stallings decided that he would get a head start on the other two boats by pushing up the River a few miles, although he knew he would have to battle a great deal of floating ice. The *Home* fought her way through to the Marcella Landing, twenty miles above Batesville. It was then midnight, and Captain Stallings decided that he would be safe in tying up his boat for the night, since he had a good twenty-mile lead on his competitors. He ordered everyone to bed except the night-watchman and instructed all to be ready to push off at five o'clock the next morning. He gave the night-watchman strict orders to have everyone awake and on the job by that hour and to keep his eyes and ears open for steamboat lights and whistles. The night-watchman assured Captain Stallings that he would give the alarm if he saw or heard any activity on the River, and the Captain went to bed feeling happy about his strategy and confident that neither Captain Smith nor Captain Woodbury would risk his boat at night in a heavy flow of ice.

About two hours later Captain Stallings was awakened by the

noise of a passing steamboat. He leaped out of bed and from his window saw the *Alberta No. 3*, the largest and fastest of the three boats driving up the River under full steam with lights blazing. He rushed about giving the alarm to officers and crew and in a few minutes had everyone awake and at his post—except the night-watchman. The Captain located him in the steward's room, reposing comfortably on two chairs and snoring with vigor and eloquence. The irate Captain kicked the chairs from under him, and the startled watchman pulled himself together and asked if the boat had run into something. He "resigned" the same day, and his resignation was accepted without undue delay. Half an hour after the *Alberta* passed, the lights of the *John F. Allen* gleamed in the distance, and she passed the *Home* before the fireman could generate a head of steam. By the time the *Home* had gone fifty miles from the Marcella landing she met the *Alberta* coming back with a full load of cotton.

With the discovery late in the century of mountains of zinc on the Buffalo River and of extensive zinc and lead deposits in neighboring areas on the White River, the future for steamboating looked never so bright. The outcome was the reverse. The railroads, too, realized the economic promise of the mineral areas on the upper White and laid a line which paralleled the River for one hundred miles, into the heart of the Ozarks.

When the railroad bed was being prepared, tons of stone were blasted from the base of the Calico Rock, and its beauty was marred. In the years since then the village that sits on top of the Rock has expanded until the dyes that once painted the bluff are gone. The ochreous clays, the acids from decaying leaves, the minerals that streaked and spotted the face of the Rock have been cut off at the source. The colors once so striking have gradually faded until the entire bluff, though still a picturesque spectacle, is now mainly black and gray. Only if through some calamity the country should return to wilderness will the Calico Rock slowly through the centuries regain its former beauty.

The railroad line was completed in 1905, and the steamboat business on the upper White received a mortal blow. With the passing of the steamboats, those noble and stately edifices with the musical whistles and bustling deck-hands, which contributed so much of the picturesque and romantic to life on the River, we suffered a grievous loss—and we are still bereft.

Chapter XI
An Appraisal

I have sometimes wondered whether growing up far back in the tall timber and in a backwoods home was, all things considered, a detriment to me. I know too well how abbreviated was my schooling and how limited were my early opportunities for broadening myself. As I have shown in the second of these sketches, my education was restricted to a few terms at subscription schools and two full-year terms at Mountain Home Academy. With the exception of schoolbooks and the Bibles there was little to read in the Leatherwoods. The Swans did not subscribe to any newspaper, and I did not see one until I was nearly fourteen years old—the *Boston Globe*, in the year 1878. There was no local newspaper, and no one in the Leatherwoods felt the need of reading metropolitan papers. Once a month when we got *Farm and Home* in the Saturday mail, we all read it through, word by word, advertisements and all, and when we reached the end we read it through again. But it could not be called an educational magazine. In 1879, when I was nearing fifteen, I saw for the first time a copy of the *Youth's Companion*, and in 1882 the *New York Ledger*, a periodical of fiction. Until I was fifteen I had never been more than ten miles from my birthplace, and at twenty-one I knew very little about our country, had never been out of the Ozark Mountains, or visited a town of more than fifteen hundred inhabitants.

On the other hand, life in the Swan home had its advantages for me. I got the necessary discipline of work and the personal discipline of a kindly man and woman who were not backward in correcting me with a switch. The scarcity of books gave all of us a greater appreciation of the few we had, and they sank much more deeply into our minds than they would otherwise have done. For this reason, I suppose, the McGuffey readers were held in almost sacred regard by the older generations of country people. (I would add that McGuffey was not afraid to use stories with a moral purpose that some day might help his readers to make sensible decisions on practical matters of importance such as everyone must face. As time has passed, pupils of McGuffey without number have had reason to be grateful for this instruction.)

I believe also that the narrow life I led during my childhood and youth has increased many times my appreciation of the world that has unfolded for me during the ensuing years. In the quiet of the hills, far from the noise and the rush of cities, I learned to look at commonplace things large and small and see whatever was special about them. And because people were scarce, everyone I saw was important—I had to know about them and get acquainted with them. Once those interests became fixed, life could never thereafter become tiresome and stale to me.

My three score years and ten have been full—a kind of journey of discovery; yet how little I know and have seen. I would have to live many times seventy years to read the books I want to read, to look into all the fields of knowledge that I think I would like, and to visit all the lands I want to see. Imagine my surprise and happiness in my young manhood when I discovered that I could understand and enjoy great writers like Dickens and Tennyson; and when I found, in reading the New York journals, that the political and social problems of Washington, New York, the nation, and even the world concerned me and that I could become well enough informed on them to talk about them with well educated people; and when I found that such a high-sounding study as archaeology was absorbing. These discoveries made me think that in some way I belonged in the big world and that though I was a raw newcomer from the backwoods I might make a place for myself in the life of the times.

My new-found interests, however, did not lessen my liking for the commonplace things that I had loved back in the hills. As an illustration I point to my interest in flowers. I began to notice them before I was six years old. This I know because I remember the flowers that grew in our yard where I lived until a short time before my sixth birthday: red, yellow, and pink zinnias, lilacs, red poppies, and coxcombs. Two vines grew along our fence, one that I later learned was a Chinese matrimony, and the other a yellow honeysuckle, very fragrant. During my nine years in the Swan home the trees, shrubs, vines, and wild flowers impressed themselves on me, and without realizing it I learned their names. I recall today the exact spot in the woods where there grew a service-berry tree, a coffee tree, a mountain ash that bloomed early in the spring, a patch of wild strawberries, a spice bush, ginseng plants, a linn tree, a slippery elm, an overcup.

In my late sixties I thought it would be interesting to transplant into my yard all the varieties of wild flowers, shrubs, and vines that I remembered from my early days on the farm. In the course of a few years I had found all but one (about seventy of them) and many others that I had not noticed or that did not grow in the Leatherwoods.

When I was in school at Spring Creek, I noticed that several of the girls in the school would sometimes paint their cheeks a beautiful coppery red, and I learned that they got the dye from the roots of a plant growing about twelve inches high on rocky, well-drained hillsides, where there was plenty of sunshine. The flowers were brilliant orange, and the plant was called Indian Paint Root (correct name: lithospermum or yellow puccoon). I had not found this plant. At length one April day as I was riding along a rolling country road, I spied on the hilly roadside a yellow-orange color that registered instantly on my mind. I got out of the car and dug up the plant by the roots, which I found no easy job, as the roots ran down deep among the rocks. Immediately I broke one of the roots and applied it to my hand. To my delight it left the coppery red stain which I had not seen in more than half a century. This flower completed my garden of the plants that I remembered from my boyhood. One of the interests of my later years has been cultivating and studying wild flowers, and many a happy afternoon I have spent in the fields and woods finding them, and at home watching them grow and bloom. Not long ago I made a list of all my growing wild shrubs, vines, and flowers and was surprised to find that it ran to about three hundred. This is but one of the enduring pleasures of my later years that I owe to my early life on the farm.

I suppose that people who were born in cities would not be able to understand why I consider myself fortunate in my birthplace and in my upbringing. My inheritance was a rich one that I would not care to give up—the blue Ozark Mountains, the crystal-clear White River with its cold tributary springs and creeks, the abundance of wild plants and animals, and above all, a good home on the frontier, and friendly neighbors. I will forever be grateful that my parents and my aunt and uncle were kind people with a sure sense of right and wrong who conscientiously tried to give me the upbringing that I needed for a happy life.

Afterword: John Q. Wolf and his Papers

In 1931 my father, John Q. Wolf, began writing random reminiscences as a means of relieving his anxiety during the long terminal illness of his wife. His intention was to publish a few of them in the local Batesville, Arkansas, newspaper for the entertainment of his fellow-townsmen. The first stories breaking into print told of amusing pranks and predicaments of two backwoods boys in a lost corner of the Ozarks. The response from readers, however, encouraged him to broaden his subject, and within a few years he was writing a series of sketches for the magazine section of the Sunday *Arkansas Gazette*, along with a variety of articles for several county papers and the *Arkansas Historical Quarterly*.

Yet he was never quite able to entertain seriously the thought of writing a book about himself, despite the suggestions of his relatives and friends. Nobody, he said, would be interested in the trivial incidents of his life except his acquaintances and the friends of the people mentioned in his stories. Occasional prodding was needed to keep him writing even the reminiscences for the newspapers; he preferred local history as a subject. In 1937, however, H. L. Mencken happened to see one of his newspaper articles and immediately wrote a complimentary letter suggesting a book on the Ozarks and offering to assist in finding a publisher. He liked the way the sketch was salted with wit and thought that a book about Ozark life written in the same not-too-serious manner would be successful. Though still incredulous, my father was much pleased by Mencken's compliment and was spurred into writing more reminiscences. Once or twice he even reached the point of discussing possible titles for a collection of sketches, but the idea of publishing a book seemed too great to him. As a consequence, he hesitated and put off making any attempt to round out or organize his material. And then it was too late.

Most of the mass of reminiscence that he wrote between 1931 and 1943 was published in the Little Rock *Arkansas Gazette*, the Batesville *Guard*, and the Batesville *News Review*, and a few other newspapers. The rest has remained in manuscript up to the present, (1971). The total number of papers that he left in his collection printed, typed, and handwritten runs into the hundreds, and there is a good deal of duplication, occasionally as many as four sketches of the same incident; but rarely are there successive drafts (first, second, etc.) of any episode. He was not interested in revision, even when the early drafts were at his elbow, but preferred to re-tell his stories for the pleasure it gave him. The different versions were usually written for different newspapers or different occasions; for example, one for the local paper (perhaps a brief sketch or single incident), one for the Mountain Home or Calico Rock weekly (in which the early citizens of Baxter and Izard counties respectively would be given prominence), one for the *Arkansas Gazette*, and one for some speaking engagement. Undertaking to edit a selection of these reminiscences, I separated all the materials relating to his first twenty-one years, clearly the most important of the manuscripts; chose the best versions or the best parts of two or more versions; combined short sketches to form chapters; and, finally, arranged the chapters in what seemed to be a reasonable order. Some of the sketches exist in only one draft, and in other cases a single version is so complete and well-finished as to need no splicing and no editing.

The indebtedness of the author to printed sources is small. He was well read in Arkansas history and owed something to the work of local historians, in particular, Augustus Curran Jeffery, whose reminiscent history of north central Arkansas appeared in the Melbourne *Clipper*, a country newspaper, in 1877. For example, his version of "Sweet Lips and Jack o' Diamonds" follows Jeffery's account, although the story was still current in the '70s and '80s. To the same historical sketch he also owed other information about the days before his birth. He doubtless read the Civil War stories of T. J. Estes, to which he refers, in some book of local history or in some county newspaper. Otherwise the contents of this volume derive from recollection and oral tradition.

Many of these sketches are descriptions of folkways, though my father made no special effort to record folklore as such. In fact, he was disinclined in his accounts of life in the Leatherwoods to attempt any use of certain kinds of it, for example, backwoods dialect—for two reasons. In the first place, he felt, mistakenly perhaps, that to put

into the mouths of his Leatherwoods friends expressions chosen sole-
ly for their quaintness might be a kind of belittlement, however
mild, or might at least set his old friends apart as a rather odd breed of
people. Another reason for his sparse use of dialect is that he had been
so much a part of mountain life that not many idioms seemed
noteworthy to him. And when, after a half-century and more, he undertook to write these sketches, most of the true backwoods expressions had faded from memory. The few that are found in this volume
were in general use in the Ozark country during the last half of the
nineteenth century.

He was also disinclined to emphasize the folkishness of the people in his sketches. Above everything else they were human beings,
never caricatures. His uncle and aunt, the parson, the schoolmaster,
the doctor, the shopkeeper, the fiddler, the postmaster, the recluse,
the politician, the farmers and their families, the officers and deck-
hands who operated the steamboats are presented as they appeared to
him, without nostalgic coloration on the one hand or emphasis on the
peculiarities of the folk on the other. Though he was forever amused
at the foibles of the people, himself most of all, he was too kind-
hearted to demean. For example, he would not use the word
roustabout when writing of the Negro deckhands because he felt that
it was somewhat deprecatory. And because of his respect for fact he
sometimes tends to underplay his story, as when he mentions, with
almost no elaboration and without show of feeling, the remarkable
fact that his aunt and uncle raised at least thirteen, or perhaps as many
as sixteen, orphan children; or when he refers with a light heart to the
threadbare diet that sustained his mother and her children during a
hard winter. If it is suspected that he exaggerated the delights of country fare, I can bear witness to the fact that during the long years when I
was with him he thought neither nature nor art offered anything better
to eat than hot biscuits and butter with molasses or honey, country
ham and black gravy, fresh fruit, rich cream, jams and preserves, and
pies—and eating was always a great pleasure to him. He could enjoy
biscuits and molasses three meals a day three hundred and sixty-five
days a year and believe that he was dining on food of the gods—but
the molasses must be choice home-made, preferably ribbon cane or
sorghum.

John Q. Wolf must be numbered among those favored souls
who find joy, the deepest kind of joy, in being alive, in living, in breathing sweet air, in drinking cold water from mountain springs, in
looking at the wonders all about them—wonders of nature, art, and

above all, human personality—listening, doing, reading, learning, sharing. He did not need to run from boredom or search for life in strange and far-off places. In a mountain trail or an abandoned field or his home library he could find endless entertainment. The commonplace no less than the unusual or awesome could stir his enthusiasm. During the Christmas season when the small wooden barrel of lady apples arrived at our house, I remember with what pleasure he opened the barrel and inhaled the good appley odor; then popped the apples as he bit into them and savored their tart, spicy juice. He lived in cheerful anticipation of tomorrow, while fully enjoying the pleasures of today. "Two weeks from now the mertensia will be in bloom!" he would say (or something of the kind), but after work-hours that afternoon he would not be able to resist going to "blood-root hill" to see if the deer-tongue was in flower, and that night he would, as like as not, be deep in *Sky and Telescope* until bedtime. More than once he remarked to me with a twinkle that he would like to become a baby and live through life again, taking his chances on what fate and circumstance might have in store for him. But I am sure he felt that in his new identity he would have his old enthusiasm for seeing and reading and exploring and learning.

In his sketches he proposed the question: was it possible for a child to grow up happily on a farm in the Ozark hills during the bleak Reconstruction period, shut out from everywhere and everything, with no regular entertainments, no toys, and little attention from anyone? Caught between hard work and the humdrum of a remote farm, how could he find life anything but wearisome? His answer is that life was full of interest, no less full than it would have been in a king's castle, because if offered something more fascinating and important than toys and gadgets and bright lights and supervised play—it offered people, not such crowds of people as cheapen a single life, but individual souls who must be identified and known. Life was good in the Leatherwoods because John was young and very much alive and because others close to him were alive and free. The setting in time and place, of course, gives his stories their color, but for him the main interest lay in the human story, the human comedy, and in the actors who deeply concerned him because they were human.

He did not realize it, but there is another important reason why his early years were happy: nature had given him a cheerful disposition and a curious and sensitive mind. Life was exciting because he was young Johnny Wolf.

My father's later profession was banking. In 1887 he located in

Batesville, Arkansas, a steamboat town in the foothills of the Ozarks, and became a partner in a banking venture that immediately prospered. In 1890 the Bank of Batesville was organized and later became the First National Bank of Batesville, with my father as ranking executive officer. He was proud of its growth and of the fact that it became the largest bank in the half of Arkansas that lies north of the Arkansas River. When the bank prospered, his cup was full; when troubles came, as come they did, he suffered.

Although he worked long and hard at the bank, his other interests were by no means forgotten. Shortly after he established a home of his own (in 1889), he did what anyone who reads these sketches might expect him to do: he began to make amends for his early privations by surrounding himself with magazines and books, on which he spent more of his income than he could well afford. His library became his principal luxury, perhaps his only one. Among my own early memories are those of the tall shelves of books in our library and of my father pulling down from the shelves some book he wanted to read to the family. On Sunday afternoons during my school years he read to me from books of his choosing. *Pickwick Papers*, which occupied us for two or three years, stands out in my memory partly because it brings to mind his chuckles and brief comments which opened the door for me to Dickens' wit. I also recall that during his summer vacation when I was ten years old, he read all of *Tom Sawyer* to my mother and me. Through the years when he came home at noon, he usually settled comfortably in his favorite chair and read the *New York Times* until called to lunch; and after the evening meal he continued with the *Times* before turning to other reading. In a college community his library was the outstanding private one and was so listed in educational surveys. Such notices, however, disturbed him because they made him appear to be a scholar and reminded him of the great difference between owning books and knowing them. A news photographer once asked him to pose for a picture in his library with an open book in his hands. He refused, saying that the picture would create a false impression and would embarrass him. Though he was more broadly educated than most college graduates, he was annoyed by his ignorance, as on every side he saw tempting fields of knowledge unknown to him and stacks of great books that reminded him of what he had not read. If he could have lived ten lives I believe that at the close, he still would have been just as eager to study and to learn.

Among his other special interests, the out-of-doors were a constant invitation to him. Color, especially the color of flowers, gave him a deep shock of pleasure. And in measure almost beyond belief he was fond of things that grow: trees, vines, shrubs, plants of all kinds. Occasionally when he walked home from downtown he would notice flowers along the way that were wilting in the hot sun. I have known him to fill a bucket with water and walk several blocks down the street to water the wilted plants. Such exceptional attention was, of course, reserved for flowers that had given him more than usual pleasure and that he hoped to see again in full bloom. In his sketches he writes of his life-long interest in wildflowers. Hundreds of times in spring, summer, fall, and winter, I have driven him to fields and woods, where with a trowel, short-handled pick, and basket, he explored for plants, and whence he always returned with a miscellaneous collection of them. He would have been pleased to ramble in the woods for an hour or more every day in the year that the weather permitted. During the long days of summer he spent almost every late afternoon walking the hillsides looking for wildflowers. Occasionally when he found an unusual show of them or a single long-sought plant, his face would light up with happiness until he would shout in an overflow of joy—and then laugh at his own folly.

He was an exceptionally close observer, and though he was never able to recognize the family automobile or to tell a Model A Ford from a Cadillac, nothing in the woods escaped his eye: the color and form of the bark on different varieties of trees, the particular way limbs branched out from the trunks of various trees, the precise shape of Kentucky coffee-bean pods, the exact hue of a wild ginger bloom.

When I became mature enough to look at my father with a degree of objectivity, I was puzzled by two questions that still baffle me. The first is why he was not permanently injured by the stultifying influences of ignorance and poverty during his childhood. The Swans owned only one book of any educational value, the Bible, and both they and the senior Wolfs were plain people of the hills with little schooling. The schools that my father attended, by and large, could not have been very good, and the five or six summer terms and the two full nine-month terms that he spent at these schools add up to little more than the three R's. Yet he was not handicapped by his meager educational experience. Neither did that other queller, poverty, crush him. His people apparently did not have at any time more money than a few head of cattle or two or three bales of cotton would bring. During one winter his mother and her children lived on corn dodgers and milk and in the spring added to this diet an assortment of wild greens. Yet he never believed that his environment was a handicap, even considered it advantageous, and at the Swans' he felt that he lived in prosperity. To him prosperity meant a strong log cabin, a farm, plenty of meat, bread and molasses, good home-spun clothes, a fireplace, a feather bed, and a family circle. In due time, he emerged quickly from this pioneer environment, as men have always done, including many in his generation and in circumstances similar to his. He did not carry away with him any enduring shackles of ignorance or bear any deep scars of privation, and in old age he looked back upon his long life as a journey of discovery.

What seeds were sown during his formative years that sprang up and flourished as he matured? What prompted the boys in the Swan home to push away from the backwoods and look with purpose for a place in the world beyond? Did the wholesome moral influences on the farm and the responsibilities placed upon them condition them for lives of usefulness in society? Did hereditary endowments stir them? Or should their ambition be attributed, at least in part, to the age of self-reliance in which they lived? On the frontier during the nineteenth century every young man was expected to assert his independence at or before age twenty-one and thereafter make his living by his own strength and skill. This responsibility was eagerly awaited and accepted without question as a test of manhood and a law of life. It was as much a part of living as being born and working and growing up. A man worth his salt would not wait for opportunity to come his way—he would create it. To get a job, to work, to raise a crop, to stand behind a counter, to set up shop, to earn money, to be one's own man, to make a place for oneself—this was independence, this was freedom, this was being a man. It may be that this compulsion, together with the encouragement of their elders, lay behind the ambitions and the successes of the likes of Walton and Wolf.

Equally puzzling to me is the intellectual curiosity of my father. In his native hills not many inspiring influences could have reached him. Was his curiosity a gift from his forebears or was his mind stimulated by the McGuffey Readers or the woodcuts in the old box of magazines at the Swans' or the color picturebook at the Hixsons', by the encouragement of his favorite teacher, Professor Kerr, or by Joshua Bond, the strange university-trained recluse, who told him unforgettable facts about the stars and the great world beyond the Leatherwood hills? Whatever its cause, my father's zest for learning was genuine and enduring. At seventy-five he was reading as eagerly as when at age eight Aunt Polly handed him the Mother Goose book.

Words fascinated him and he enjoyed turning them over on his tongue. Throughout the years, even into old age, he committed to memory a considerable number of poems, which he was fond of reciting during leisure moments at home, all of them good poems written by men who knew their craft. The favorite author of his last years was T. E. Lawrence, whose works were not to be read and laid aside, but re-read and re-enjoyed with friends. One reason for the appeal of *Revolt in the Desert* was its connection with the Near-East, long a favorite subject of study. For fifty years he had read of the archaeological work in that area, and he sometimes carried in his coat pocket one or two small baked tablets from excavations in the Tigris-Euphrates country. These he enjoyed showing to his friends with explanations of where they were found and what their purport was. Toward the end of his life he remarked more than once as he looked back over the past that one of his greatest regrets was that he had not read more good literature, and he mentioned in particular his meager knowledge of Shakespeare—as though he had missed too much of life. I find it equally unaccountable that as a farm boy he should have cared enough about wild flowers (weeds) to learn their names, and as a man to build an outstanding collection of them in his yard. There may be answers to these questions, but I do not know them. My father was and remains to me an enigma.

During the century that has passed since my father was a small boy, the Leatherwoods Country has changed remarkably little. It is still a picturesque and unspoiled bit of the frontier, and the untroubled peace and quiet of the hills still hang over it. The cold springs still gush from the hillsides, and the clear mountain streams flow through it as swiftly as they did a hundred years ago. The 1970 census gives the population of Stone County as only 6,830, a gain of 544 over 1960, and the county seat and largest town, Mountain View, now claims 1,866 inhabitants. Farming remains the principal occupation, but the domestic system, the practice of "raising a living," was abandoned long ago. The ancient arts and crafts of spinning, weaving, soap-making, candle-molding and the like have not been lost, however, and at folk festivals and on other special occasions the craftsmen gather and display their wares. The cabin of the Swans still stands, although its logs have been covered with weather-boards; and the schoolhouse at Spring Creek, where Professor Kerr taught the three R's for several years, is still there. But a few of the old mountain trails have become hard-surfaced roads, and a bridge now spans the White River where the old ferry used to run at Calico Rock.

During the next decade parts of Stone County will undergo far more radical changes than these—changes so great that much of it cannot long remain a land of open spaces and calm, unhurried living. Two federal projects are certain to make Stone County a tourist attraction visited annually by hundreds of thousands of people. The first is the building of a folk-arts center at Mountain View, with auditorium, library, exhibition rooms, and facilities for studying various kinds of native folklore. This project grew out of the annual folk festival and arts-crafts exhibit at Mountain View, a four-day event that features native folk artists and musicians and draws thousands of visitors.

The second project is the development by the federal government of the Blanchard Springs Caverns, a vast underground showplace, on which millions of dollars have already been spent, with millions yet to come. Government sources estimate that half a million tourists will visit the Caverns the first year they are open to the public. As a result of these two developments, southern Stone County will soon swarm with motels, restaurants, roadside hamburger and hot-dog bars, and all the litter that goes with crowds of people on vacation. The natives even more than the countryside are certain to change. They cannot maintain their folkways honestly and pursue their folk culture except in remoteness from urban crowds, urban money, and urban jobs. As of 1970, however, Stone County is still unspoiled. And the Leatherwoods, which rise twenty miles to the north of these projects, may feel only slightly the impact of change.

John Quincy Wolf, Jr.
Memphis, 1971

ONE

BAXTI

MARION

Lead Hill

Eli.vir

Oregon

Doddsville

Mountain Home

Glenwood

Whiteville

Crooked Cr.

Georges Creek

Gassville

Big Pond

Pleasant Ridge

Bellefonte

Yellville

Buford

Lone Ro

Rally Hill

Clear Cr.

ey Springs

Eros

Rosslow

Gaitherville

shall Prairie

Water Creek

Duggers Mills

Cit

Wells Cr.

Wells Creek

Saint Joe

Tomahawk C.

Buffalo Fork

Mount Hersey

Mill C.

Tomahawk

Big Flat

of White R.

ed Rock

Pt. Peter

SEARCY

De Soto

Providence

ON

Cave Cr.

Calf Creek

Marshall

t. Judea

Big C.

Richland C.

Calf Cr.

Bear C.

Alco

S

Bear Creek

Wileys Cove

Blue Mountain

Owl Fork

Witts Springs

Turkey C

Oak Flat

Little Red

Middle Fork

Freeman

Mid

Geesville

Clinton

Eglantin

VAN BUREN

South Fk.

Liberty Springs

Scotland

Scottsville

Glass Village

Rondo

Bee Branc

OPE

Appleton

Dover

Caglesville

Lick Mountain

Moreland

Center Ridge

Gum Log

Isabella

Old Hickory

North Fk. Cadron C.

CONWAY

ussellville

Potts Sta. P.O.

Galla Cr. Sta.

Blackville

Rene. C.

Solgohachia

Springfield

Greenb

rristown

M